DECORATING with
FABRIC

DECORATING with FABRIC

Hundreds of ideas for window treatments,
bed linens, pillows, slipcovers and lampshades

KATE FRENCH & KATHERINE SORRELL

with photography by LISA COHEN

RYLAND PETERS & SMALL
LONDON • NEW YORK

DESIGNER Pamela Daniels

SENIOR EDITOR Henrietta Heald

LOCATION RESEARCH Jess Walton

PRODUCTION Gordana Simakovic

ART DIRECTOR Leslie Harrington

PUBLISHING DIRECTOR Alison Starling

STYLING Kate French

TEXT Katherine Sorrell

Originally published in 2008 as *Fabric Inspirations*.
This revised edition published in 2020 by
Ryland Peters & Small
20–21 Jockey's Fields
London WC1R 4BW
and
Ryland Peters & Small, Inc.
341 E 116th Street
New York, NY 10029
www.rylandpeters.com

10 9 8 7 6 5 4 3 2 1
Text, design and photographs copyright
© Ryland Peters & Small 2008, 2020

ISBN: 978-1-78879-184-7

A CIP record for this book is available from the British Library.

Library of Congress CIP data has been applied for.

PRINTED IN CHINA

CONTENTS

INTRODUCTION

It is hard to imagine a beautiful home that doesn't make inspirational use of fabrics. The fabrics could be wildly luxurious or chic-but-cheap; they could be minimal and neutral or colourful and dramatic; they could be frivolous and fun or just superbly functional. Fabrics can be used in all sorts of ways, and are vital to the success of any decorative scheme, setting the overall style, disguising bad points or highlighting good ones and, of course, bringing softness, warmth and character.

From a practical point of view, fabrics keep us warm, help us to sit and lie comfortably, protect delicate surfaces and provide privacy and shade. Weaving was one of primitive humanity's earliest crafts, and the basic principle of interwoven warp and weft have changed little, if at all, since the days of sixth-century warp-weighted looms. But, these days, fabrics are much more than just a bare necessity; they are tactile and colourful, as well as beautiful to look at and to live with. Whether your style is sophisticated or relaxed, traditional or modern, fabrics can help create a home that is individual, comfortable and timelessly appealing.

Decorating with Fabric looks in turn at all the main rooms of the home – living rooms, bedrooms, kitchens and dining rooms, even home offices and bathrooms – and also at outdoor spaces, including terraces, patios, summerhouses and gardens. In some spaces fabrics are used extensively; in others, less so – but in all cases their contribution is fundamental.

The book focuses on the key ways in which fabrics are used in each space – whether it be as window treatments, upholstery, bed linen, table linens, awnings or accessories – and compares the different options available; it considers which fabrics might work best (and which really wouldn't), suggests clever ways of saving money, time and effort, and considers a range of stylistic possibilities.

The photographs were taken in the homes of fabric connoisseurs – people who know how to use fabrics with flair and creativity but also understand the practical requirements of everyday life. The majority of their ideas are satisfyingly simple and easy to emulate – perhaps just an elegant curtain made from crisp linen in a deep, plain colour, a cushion with luxurious silk fringing or a chair cover made from loosely fitted, washable cotton. Others are more complicated, and might need a little extra personal input. Even on the smallest budget, however, it should be possible to take inspiration from the ingenious ideas and down-to-earth suggestions that are included in the following pages. This is not simply a good-looking book designed to be thumbed through and put down. It contains plenty of information that will help in real-life situations, whether you live in the country or the city, own a spacious home or a tiny one, have children or pets, are short of time or have little spare cash. The starting points are all here; the rest is up to you.

choosing fabric

COLOUR

Daring and dynamic or mellow and muted, colour is often the element that, beyond all others, defines the character of a room. A versatile and effective tool, it can influence the way we react to an environment both emotionally and physically. There are even colour clichés – for example, the teenager's bedroom that is completely black; the seaside bathroom in blue and yellow; and the white-on-white home of a design purist.

OPPOSITE TOP ROW Bold colours are not to everyone's taste, but with judicious use they can look fantastic. A set of cushions, for example, could be made from plain cotton in varying acid shades (far left), and perhaps trimmed with matching ric rac, ribbon or bobbles (centre). Deep blues (right) are dramatic but also calming and sophisticated.

OPPOSITE BOTTOM ROW, LEFT TO RIGHT Use varying tones of the same colour for a scheme that looks hugely effective but is actually relatively simple to put together. Luscious pinks and reds make a vibrant combination. These cushions, from Marijke van Nunen, employ a range of vivid colours that work really well together and are offset by the white sofa.

RIGHT A good fabric retailer such as London's Cloth House will have a choice of specialist fabrics and an enormous selection of luxury and everyday fabrics, in a rainbow of colours.

What, then, are the secrets of putting together a fabric colour scheme that expresses your personality, works with the architecture of your home, suits your existing furnishings, makes you feel good and, above all, fits in with the way you live? It probably makes sense to consider the last point first. For example, if there are young children or pets in your household, then white or very pale upholstery is likely to be out of the question, although you could possibly get away with washable slipcovers. Pale curtains, too, show the dirt more readily than darker ones, so make allowances for more frequent cleaning – or else avoid them entirely.

ABOVE White upholstery looks crisp and chic, especially in combination with taupe walls and dark woodwork. Sequinned cushions, in white-on-white, are suitably neutral but add a pretty, informal touch.

ABOVE RIGHT These neutrally toned cushions and throw were traditionally woven at Melin Tregwynt wool mill in Wales. The geometric patterns are retro in style but modern in interpretation.

With the practicalities sorted out, think about which colour ranges you naturally prefer. Broadly, colours can be divided into neutrals, pastels and brights. Most of us gravitate unconsciously towards one end of the spectrum rather than the other, and the colour choices we make are usually based on a combination of hard logic and pure emotion.

Consider which colours would work best with the furniture you already possess. You may want to have colours that complement your existing things or to create dramatic contrasts, such as matching pale linens with dark wood. Do your preferred colours feel right with the architecture of the property? In some older houses, modern colours – such as brilliant white, a 20th-century invention – look wrong (although there is also much to be said for the careful juxtaposition of old and new). Do your colours show off the spaces to best

advantage? Pale colours seem to recede, enhancing the sense of space, while darker colours absorb light and appear more enclosing. Similarly, 'cool' colours such as blue and green are more distancing than 'warm' colours such as red and yellow. That is why paler, cooler colours work well in small rooms, and warmer colours are particularly effective in rooms that receive only northern or eastern light.

Colour inspiration can be found in books and magazines, in the natural world and, most straightforwardly, in manufacturers' fabric books. When making a decision, look at the fabric in situ (ask for a swatch or a longer, returnable length) and in the type of light in which it will most often be seen. Taking all these considerations into account, follow your instincts and choose colours that you really love and that you can't wait to live with.

ABOVE WHEN USING NEUTRALS, TEXTURE BECOMES INCREASINGLY IMPORTANT. COMBINING ROUGH WITH SMOOTH, NUBBLY WITH SHINY, OR HAIRY WITH SLEEK INTRODUCES AN EXTRA ELEMENT TO A SCHEME THAT GIVES IT GENUINE LIFE AND SOUL. THESE SUMPTUOUS CUSHIONS ARE FROM ATELIER ABIGAIL AHERN.

ABOVE LEFT A BOLD DASH OF COLOUR, SUCH AS THIS MUSTARD YELLOW, ADDS ZING TO AN OTHERWISE UNDERSTATED SCHEME.

PATTERN

After years in which designers have favoured cool, understated home interiors, pattern has come into its own again. And pattern, like colour, can be a wonderful addition to a home, giving character, drama and vitality. From the subtlest of stripes to the most striking of modern floral prints, whether it is used boldly over large expanses or in small doses as a counterpoint to plains, pattern offers choices to suit any space.

OPPOSITE, TOP ROW, LEFT TO RIGHT THIS OPEN FLORAL HAS A CHARMING NOSTALGIC QUALITY. IT WOULD BE EFFECTIVE AS UPHOLSTERY, CURTAINS OR CUSHIONS – THOUGH PERHAPS NOT ALL AT ONCE. DURABLE COTTON TICKING IS AN IDEAL FABRIC FOR COVERING SEAT CUSHIONS. AS WELL AS STRENGTHENING THE COVERS, THE PIPED/CORDED EDGES ADD A CHIC FINISHING TOUCH. WHEN CHOOSING PATTERNS, UNROLL LENGTHS OF FABRIC AND DRAPE THEM AROUND THE SHOWROOM TO GET A GOOD IMPRESSION OF THEIR OVERALL EFFECT.

OPPOSITE, BOTTOM ROW, LEFT TO RIGHT THESE TICKING CHAIR COVERS ARE SIMPLE, CHEAP AND APPEALING. A SHEER WITH A SOFTLY ABSTRACT, GEOMETRIC PATTERN IS DELICATE AND PRETTY. A TEA TOWEL/DISHTOWEL WITH WIDE-APART STRIPES MAKES A LOVELY TABLECLOTH.

RIGHT THIS MODERN FLORAL FABRIC HAS A FEMININE FEEL WITHOUT BEING EXCESSIVELY FLOUNCY OR FUSSY.

Start by deciding what kind of patterns you like. Are you drawn to simple, graphic motifs in muted colours or naturalistic designs in vivid shades? Is your preference for large-scale or small-scale designs? For historical or modern representations? And would you like just a dash of a single pattern to enliven an otherwise plain room or a striking combination of patterns for an all-over look? There are several things to take into account. The first is colour. When mixing patterns or combining a patterned fabric with a plain one, a really good colour match is important. This will draw the different elements together to create a unified effect. The second is scale. In bigger

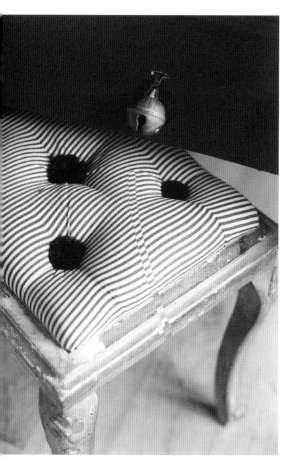

rooms, you can afford to use very large-scale patterns for impact, while smaller rooms are generally better suited to medium- or small-scale patterns – unless you want to make a particular feature out of a tiny room by blasting it with a giant pattern. When combining patterns, aim to vary their scales without going to extremes. Very small patterns are only really noticeable close up; from a distance they look like a plain colour. Although this can be a disappointment, it may also be an advantage, since a tiny pattern can be used as a lovely addition to a scheme that needs a decorative but subtle element. The third consideration is density. Loose, open patterns give a visual 'breather', while intricate patterns with closely placed designs have more drama. When several patterns are used together, a variety of densities gives balance and interest. Finally, remember that pattern combinations are best confined to designs that originate from the same era or stylistic aesthetic.

You may own the perfect pattern inspiration already: an antique quilt, a painted vase, a print from an old book, a favourite shirt. Consult magazines and books for further ideas, and borrow ideas from other people's homes, or even from fashionable bars, restaurants or shops. Mixing patterns can be as simple as choosing a floral and a stripe in one colourway from a single manufacturer, or it may involve more time and effort spent on putting together just the right elements from a variety of sources.

ABOVE STRIPES ARE TIMELESS AND ALWAYS LOOK CHIC, AS WELL AS BEING EASY TO COMBINE WITH OTHER PATTERNS. HERE, POM-POM BUTTONS ADD AN AMUSING TOUCH.

RIGHT FOR A SUCCESSFUL MIX OF MODERN AND ANTIQUE FLORALS, TRY TO MATCH THE COLOURS AND THE SCALE OF THE PATTERNS.

FAR RIGHT YOU CAN USE REMNANTS OF PATTERNED FABRIC TO GIVE EVERYDAY OBJECTS A LUXURIOUS FEEL.

OPPOSITE THIS BOLD COMBINATION WORKS BECAUSE THE AESTHETIC IS SO CLEAR: THE COLOURS ARE COMPLEMENTARY AND THE PATTERNS HAVE A SIMILARLY GRAPHIC NATURE.

TEXTURE

The way a space feels is as important as the way it looks. Colours and patterns may be the first things you notice when you walk into a room, but the more time you spend in it, the more prominent textures become. They can make you feel comfortably at home or inexplicably ill at ease; this is not surprising when you consider that an appreciation of texture allows us to relate to our surroundings in a direct and sensual way.

OPPOSITE, TOP ROW, LEFT TO RIGHT TIGHTLY WOVEN LINEN MAKES FABULOUS UPHOLSTERY AND HAS A UNIQUE FEEL THAT IS CRISP, COOL AND VERY APPEALING. NO-NONSENSE COTTON TICKING IS INEXPENSIVE AND WORKS WELL AS AN ALL-ROUND TEXTURE. A SWATHE OF SEQUINS GIVES THIS CUSHION A GLAMOROUS AIR.

OPPOSITE, BOTTOM ROW, LEFT TO RIGHT COTTON CAN BE WOVEN INTO A RANGE OF WEIGHTS AND TEXTURES, FROM CHEESECLOTH TO CANVAS. THIS THROW BY VOLGA LINEN COMBINES MERINO WOOL AND CRISP LINEN FOR A WONDERFUL TEXTURAL CONTRAST. SOFT VELVET IS SUMPTUOUS FOR CURTAINS AND GORGEOUS TO SINK INTO ON A SOFA.

RIGHT THESE BLANKETS AND THROWS ARE KNITTED AND WOVEN FROM DIFFERENT FIBRES, RESULTING IN A STRONG TEXTURAL CONTRAST, DESPITE THE SIMILARITIES OF COLOUR, THAT IS BOTH GOOD-LOOKING AND APPEALING.

A fabric's texture is determined by the type of fibre from which it is made and the way in which the yarn has been spun; it is also affected by the type of weave (plain, ribbed, twill, satin or pile, for example) and density of yarns used. This means that there is an enormous variety of fabric textures to choose from: cotton, for example, can be constructed so that it becomes fluffy terry towelling, stiff canvas, open cheesecloth or soft velvet. And, from the harsh shininess of horsehair to the ultra-soft give of cashmere, from the crispness of linen to the homely warmth of felted wool, an imaginative use of textured fabrics can undoubtedly bring a room to life.

ABOVE ROLLED-UP LENGTHS OF LINEN
DEMONSTRATE HOW SOFT AND TACTILE THIS
FABRIC CAN BE. A NEUTRAL COLOUR SUCH AS
THIS COULD BE USED FOR SHEETS, CURTAINS,
UPHOLSTERY OR TABLECLOTHS. IT WOULD
ALSO TAKE DYE VERY EASILY.

OPPOSITE THE VIVID ORANGE PIPING ON THIS
CURTAIN BY MARIJKE VAN NUNEN SERVES TO
ACCENTUATE THE DIFFERENT WEIGHTS OF THE
TWO LINENS FROM WHICH IT IS MADE.

To create an interesting, enjoyable, harmonious combination of textures, it is advisable to begin with the basics. Aim to decorate your home with upholstery or slipcovers in a fabric that is neither so shiny and slippery that you slide off it the moment you sit down, nor so nubbly and rough that it is uncomfortable and liable to snag instantly. Look for curtains that draw easily, table linen that can safely be put in the washing machine, bed linen that feels good against the skin, and so on.

A 'quiet', fairly smooth texture is, therefore, likely to be the backbone of most schemes, but the interest it adds to a room depends totally on how it is combined and contrasted with other elements. Think of layering one texture with another, then perhaps adding touches of one or two more. The aim is to achieve pleasing contrasts rather than clashes, so avoid too many unusual textures in one space – it is a matter of trims and accents rather than focal points. A woollen throw, for example, could be given an edging of silk satin, while a plain cotton sofa could be piled with velvet or lace cushions. A linen curtain could have a deep border in taffeta or tweed, while a tablecloth could consist of a sheer and an opaque fabric for a layered effect.

You can incorporate other elements, too, such as hide, fur, feathers, lace, buttons, appliqué, embroidery, knitting or crochet, and there are even more exciting possibilities – a feather edging around a lampshade, perhaps, or a set of embroidered napkins – resulting in textural contrasts that are practical and intuitive, nurturing and sophisticated, intriguing and full of delight.

FUNCTION

When you are choosing fabrics for any project, the key factors to think about are budget, personal taste and the overall decoration of the room, but there are other things to consider too. From a practical point of view, it is vital to match the fabric well to its intended use. No fabric does everything, but the trick – particularly if you are spending a lot of money – is to ensure that you get absolutely the best out of it.

OPPOSITE Choosing the right fabric for the purpose and place for which it's required is important. A knowledgeable retailer will be able to offer invaluable advice on issues such as durability, weight, laundering or special treatments, and also on linings and backings, how to combine two or more fabrics, and all sorts of other points. All the fabrics shown here are from London's Cloth House, which sells an enormous range of both everyday and innovative fabrics.

RIGHT For a utilitarian kitchen screen, elaborate fabric is best avoided in favour of a plain and simple cloth, which sews easily, washes well and can be replaced inexpensively when necessary.

Durability is usually a high priority when choosing fabric, particularly when the fabric will be used for upholstery, slipcovers or curtains, since they tend to be the most expensive items to replace. Fabric is divided into various categories depending on whether it will be subjected to light, general or heavy domestic use. Certain types of fabric and weave will survive more wear than others – and while, in general, heavier weights and tighter weaves are the longest-lasting, it is not always possible to tell just by looking. Your supplier should be able to provide details of how well your chosen fabric performed in tests, and to advise on its suitability for your project. Weight is another issue. Heavier fabrics may be too bulky for small projects, while lighter fabrics may be too flimsy for more

ambitious ones. Take roman blinds, for example: too light a fabric would not hang well, while too heavy a fabric would not gather into neat folds. For curtains, the larger they are the heavier the fabric should be, although a light fabric can be lined and interlined so that it hangs well and provides proper heat and light insulation.

Size matters, at least for any major project. When buying new fabric for curtains, upholstery or slipcovers, table linen or bed linen, bear in mind that the greater the width the better the value, and the less sewing that will be required. Ease of cleaning is important too. Check whether the fabric is pre-shrunk and, if not, how much it is likely to shrink when washed. Is it machine-washable, and at what temperature? And even if it is, does your washing machine have the capacity to cope with a potentially large and unwieldy curtain or slipcover?

Finally, there are some areas of the home for which you need to select a specific type of fabric or to have the fabric that you have chosen specially treated. For furniture and cushions that are intended for use outdoors or in a damp and steamy bathroom – or maybe even in a kitchen or conservatory – waterproof or at least mildew-resistant fabrics are desirable. For upholstery and slipcovers, fire-retardant fabrics are advisable (in certain cases, they are a legal requirement), and in a busy household, with pets and children, stain-resistant finishes can be a wonderful idea for much-used seat covers.

ABOVE These relaxed floor cushions are made from old kilim rugs, backed in heavy cotton. The contrast blanket stitching adds a lovely finishing touch.

RIGHT Good fabric stockists offer an enormous choice, not just in terms of fibres, weaves, colours and patterns, but also with regard to widths, weights and treatments such as pre-shrinking.

FAR RIGHT A tweed blanket is a warm and cosy throw, but the velvet edging makes it more luxurious.

THIS PAGE TEXTURE IS THE KEY ELEMENT
OF THIS ROOM. THE SQUARE-SHAPED SOFA
IS UPHOLSTERED IN AN UNUSUAL HEMP
FABRIC WITH A DISTINCTIVE WEAVE. IT IS
ADORNED WITH CUSHION COVERS MADE
FROM VINTAGE GRAIN SACKS AND
A CASHMERE THROW.

the rooms

LIVING ROOMS

Fabrics breathe life into a living room, creating a
beautiful backdrop for entertaining, listening to
music, reading, chatting or simply doing nothing.
Choose sophisticated plains or attractive patterns,
can't-keep-your-hands-off textures and delightful,
imaginative details for a room that is tranquil,
comfortable and irresistibly inviting.

'What is fashionable in contemporary interiors is a careful combination of plain/solid fabrics and subtle patterns, incorporating interesting textures and eye-catching details.'

Fabrics enhance the tactile quality of a living room to an enormous degree. The living room is the space that offers a safe haven after a hard day's work, somewhere to snuggle up for the evening on a cosy sofa, with thick curtains drawn against the dark world outside. Propped up on a pile of cushions, you might feel like wrapping yourself up in a soft throw or stretching out your legs on an upholstered footstool.

A living room can take on a variety of personalities, however. At night it may be a relaxing retreat or the setting for an uproarious party; during the day it may be transformed into a children's playroom or a home office. Before making any decisions about fabrics, think about how the room is used, and by whom. In a hard-working family living room, tough (and washable) fabrics are a necessity, whereas in living rooms that are reserved for adults only, or used only on special occasions, more delicate fabrics may be an option.

Since sofa covers and large curtains are expensive to replace, be careful to choose colours, patterns and textures that will stand the test of time. Ephemeral fabric fashions are best reserved for accessories such as cushions, lampshades and throws, which can be changed easily and cheaply. That said, it isn't always necessary to spend a fortune on curtains and upholstery – buy masses of inexpensive cotton or linen and use it generously as curtains, or make it up really well as slipcovers (complete with piped edges and carefully finished valances/ruffles), and it will look absolutely fine.

Painstaking matching of soft furnishings is no longer *de rigueur* (thank goodness). What is fashionable in contemporary interiors is a careful combination of plain/solid fabrics and subtle patterns, incorporating interesting textures and eye-catching details such as trims and borders. Certainly, if walls are patterned, it is advisable to choose fabrics that are, on the whole, relatively subtle and muted. On the other hand, if walls and floor are plain, a fabulously dramatic fabric may be just the thing for a curtain or sofa, providing a joyful focal point that, with any luck, will give you pleasure for years to come.

WINDOW TREATMENTS

Window treatments keep in the warmth and keep out prying eyes, but they are much more than a purely practical addition to a living room. A well-designed set of curtains or blinds can complement the room's architecture, disguise a poorly proportioned window or a terrible view, filter bright light, provide a visual link between inside and out and, in general, give the room a satisfyingly 'finished' feel.

Usually considered the luxurious choice for living-room windows, curtains can be made in a wide range of styles, from the utterly minimal to the lavish and ornate. How a curtain hangs – and thus its overall appearance – is determined by its heading, usually created by a tape which is sewn onto the back of the curtain and pulled to form pleats, gathers, goblets or other shapes. For a less formal look, tab-tops and tie-tops (often found on ready-made curtains), are pretty, though they can be fiddly to draw. Curtains can also be hung from a deep hem or large eyelets, both of which are simply slid over a pole, from clips (magnetic ones are easy to use) or even – for complete simplicity in a very informal room – from hooks.

Poles and tracks can be chosen either to make an impact or for their ability to disappear into the background. Made from metal, plastic, wood, bamboo, acrylic or glass, fixed or extending, straight or bent to fit around bays, they are available in all sorts of sizes, styles and colours, and can, if you wish, be fitted with finials to complement the curtain fabric and the decoration elsewhere in the room. On narrow windows or dormers, portière

LEFT A LIGHT CURTAIN, IN A FABRIC DESIGNED BY SASHA WADDELL FOR TEED INTERIORS, BRINGS INFORMALITY TO A CLASSIC ROOM.

OPPOSITE, BELOW LEFT AND CENTRE
TIE-TOP CURTAINS CONSIST OF A HEMMED RECTANGLE OF FABRIC WITH PAIRS OF TIES SEWN AT INTERVALS ALONG THE TOP EDGE. HERE, THEY HAVE BEEN MADE EXTRA LONG TO DRAPE ON THE FLOOR, CLEVERLY OFFSETTING THE STARKNESS OF THE BLACK-AND-WHITE SCHEME. THIS LINEN IS IN A PATTERN CALLED DANDELION, BY BORDERLINE.

(or swing-arm) rods are an alternative to fixed poles, while for a contemporary effect tension wire, fixed taut within the window opening, is a barely there option.

To allow maximum light to come into the room, fit a pole or track that overhangs far enough on each side to allow the curtains to be drawn right away from the window. Remember that very full, thick curtains need more 'stack back' space than light, thin ones. If there is space on one side only, fit a single curtain. Floor-length curtains are more fashionable than sill-length ones these days, although there are occasions when shorter curtains are either more practical or suit the space better (when radiators or window seats are in the way, for example). In-between lengths can look odd, unless they have been specifically designed to disguise awkward window proportions.

Tracks can be fitted with a pull cord to avoid handling the fabric every time the curtains are drawn. Alternatively, a low-tech solution is to use a rod, which hangs from the leading ring of each curtain (suitable with either tracks or poles), while the high-tech answer is an electric system, which could be operated by a switch or remote control, and even programmed to operate at pre-set times. Follow the manufacturer's recommendations as to the weight of fabric that can be pulled by the system.

Curtains can be made from practically any fabric, from cotton or linen to silk or wool. The heavier the fabric, the better it will hold a fold, though very heavy fabrics will be too bulky for smaller windows. Very light fabrics tend to look floppy, unless supported by a lining. Pure, crisp linen looks gorgeous; if you can't afford it new, keep an eye out at auctions and in second-hand

shops for linen sheets, which can be headed, hemmed and hung without great difficulty. Cotton–linen mixes are a great choice, offering a combination of function and looks that's hard to beat. Cotton velvet is opulent, hangs well and comes in wonderful colours, as does silk, which is available in a wide range of weights and finishes. Consider less conventional fabrics and weaves, from fleece to felt, cashmere to canvas, towelling to tweed. And think laterally about where to obtain fabric: flat sheets, tablecloths or large old curtains can all be reworked into new curtains or blinds, and blankets, quilts, saris, old lace panels and lightweight rugs can look beautiful when hung in the right places.

Once regarded as a poor relation to curtains, blinds are now fashionable, offering a clean-lined look that is sophisticated and laid-back yet pleasingly tactile. What's more, they tend to be far cheaper, since they need much less fabric – just the size of the window opening, plus hems. Roller blinds, the minimalist option, tend to be too utilitarian for most living rooms, though can be used as a functional window dressing (for privacy, perhaps) to complement a set of curtains. Roll-up blinds are almost as simple, but have a prettier look, tied with coordinating tape or ribbon, while roman blinds, which fold up into

ABOVE This monochromatic roll-up blind was designed by Tapet-Café, using a silk-and-banana-leaf fabric by Andrew Martin.

RIGHT In the living room of interior designer Rose Uniacke, sumptuous full-length silk curtains screen a bay window. The metal track was specially made to fit.

OPPOSITE The neutral, subtly toning colour scheme in this New York apartment is complemented by a translucent roman blind, specially made to fit the wide window. The pale blind provides privacy while doing little to block out the light.

neat, wide pleats, are a chic option and suit most styles of room. Mid-weight, not-too-textured fabrics tend to be best for blinds, which need to roll or fold easily against themselves. Both blinds and curtains can be made in more than one type of fabric, with borders at the sides or along the bottom in a contrasting colour or texture to the main fabric. Make sure the two fabrics are of a similar weight, though, or they will hang awkwardly.

Even the plainest of blinds can be embellished with the addition of a good-looking pull, which could be in an interesting shape or made from an unusual material such as leather, glass, raffia, stone or rope, while any window dressing can be given an amusing twist with ribbons, pom poms, ric rac, stitching, fringing or another trim.

SLIPCOVERS & UPHOLSTERY

Tailored or relaxed, plain or patterned, furniture that has been upholstered or slipcovered is a very important element of any living room, and the fabric you choose for the purpose will have as much impact on the appearance of the entire space as any window treatments. From a practical point of view, hard-wearing, tightly woven

ABOVE THIS OVERSIZED SOFA BY JOB INTERIEUR HAS A SIMPLE LINEN COVER.

ABOVE CENTRE FOR COMFORT ON A CHILLY EVENING, IT'S HARD TO BEAT PULLING A SOFT THROW OVER YOU WHILE SNUGGLING ON A COSY SOFA OR ARMCHAIR. THIS ONE IS CASHMERE, FROM ROSE UNIACKE'S ROSE COLLECTION.

ABOVE RIGHT A SLIPCOVER CAN TRANSFORM A TIRED SOFA. WASHABLE FABRICS ARE A PRACTICAL CHOICE WHEN USING PALE COLOURS. THIS PRETTY CUSHION IS IN SASHA WADDELL'S FLORAL CHIC FABRIC FOR TEED INTERIORS.

OPPOSITE IN THIS RESTFUL ROOM, VINTAGE MOROCCAN WEDDING BLANKETS, WITH DEEPLY FRINGED EDGES, ARE USED AS RUGS AND HAVE BEEN MADE INTO CUSHIONS. THE ARMRESTS OF THE SOFA ARE MADE FROM PILED-UP LINEN CUSHIONS FILLED WITH LAVENDER.

fabrics that are neither too rough nor too slippery are particularly well suited to most upholstery and slipcovers. Medium- to heavy-weight cottons and cotton mixes, linen mixes and wools are all good choices, while corduroy, moleskin and low-pile velvet are interesting and, because they are thick and soft, delightfully comfortable. Avoid deep piles, which may become crushed, and loose or loopy weaves, which are likely to snag. Remember to relate the weight of the fabric to the size and shape of the piece being covered – a thick, heavy tweed would be wrong on a small, fine seat cover, for example, while a fine, light fabric would appear too fragile on a large sofa.

For both new and replacement upholstery and slipcovers, whatever fabric you choose should usually be fire-retardant, though it is sometimes possible to use just a fire-retardant interlining. Always ask the manufacturer or retailer for safety advice.

Plain/solid fabrics are a sophisticated choice for upholstery and slipcovers, and can make plenty of impact with lovely textures and details such as piping/cording, buttoning and valances/dust ruffles. For disguising dirt and wear and tear, however, patterns are generally recommended – even the

ABOVE CHOCOLATE-LINEN UPHOLSTERY COMPLEMENTS THE MOODY TONES IN THIS APARTMENT DESIGNED BY JOB INTERIEUR. THE CURTAINS ARE ALSO MADE FROM LINEN, WHILE THE PAINT THAT HAS BEEN USED TO COVER THE WALLS HAS A SOFT, CHALKY TEXTURE.

ABOVE RIGHT TEXTURE IS A KEY ELEMENT OF THIS LIVING ROOM. THE CLEAN-LINED ARMCHAIR IS UPHOLSTERED IN AN UNUSUAL HEMP FABRIC WITH A DISTINCTIVE WEAVE; IT HAS A LINEN CUSHION AND A WOVEN CASHMERE BLANKET BY ROSE UNIACKE.

most subtle damask can help to disguise sticky fingerprints or paw marks. Checks and stripes can look wonderful, too, though they should be carefully aligned in order to look their best.

An imaginative way to cover an informal sofa is to use several different (but very well-coordinated) patterns together – so you may have a stripe for the back, a check for the seat and a floral fabric for the arms, for example. This conveys a sort of boho-chic effect that is most successful when other fabrics in the room either echo one of the patterns used or are in complementary plains/solids.

When you are choosing patterns for furniture covers, relate their scale carefully to the piece that is being covered and, if you choose a bold pattern, bear in mind that large motifs may look strange unless they are centred on sofa or chair backs, so you will need to buy more fabric to be confident that

everything will fit properly in the right place. This may also be relevant when you are using fabrics that feature pile (such as velvet or velour), nap (such as suedecloth), a 'float' (such as satin) or a ridge (such as corduroy), since they will need to be made up running in the same direction just as carefully as a more obvious pattern.

The styles of both fixed covers and slipcovers can vary from the perfectly tailored to the casually comfortable. By using piping/cording, pleating and, in the case of upholstery, buttoning, you can create a formal, traditional effect, while gathers and – for slipcovers – ties and a relaxed fit are more laissez-faire. Deep ruffles have 'country' associations, while scallop-edged valances are rather old-fashioned; the good news is that it's relatively easy to have a new slipcover made that will completely transform the proportions and character of a sofa or chair, however out of date its upholstery.

ABOVE Details often make all the difference when it comes to upholstery. This armchair, in an unusual pleated fabric by Rose Uniacke, features subtle buttoning on the arms.

ABOVE LEFT Velvet sofas are soft and cuddly to sink into. In this room, the sofa by George Smith complements cushions in a mix of felt, hemp, linen and knitted wool from Atelier Abigail Ahern.

BELOW, CLOCKWISE FROM TOP LEFT

A BEAUTIFUL PIECE OF ANTIQUE LACE SETS OFF THIS DISPLAY TO ELEGANT EFFECT. ALL THE OBJECTS ARE FROM VINTAGE BY NINA. RENOWNED MID-20TH CENTURY DESIGNER FLORENCE BROADHURST COMBINED VIBRANT COLOURS AND DYNAMIC FORMS. TEXTURES TAKE OVER IN THIS PILE OF VINTAGE LACE AND MOROCCAN WEDDING BLANKETS. THESE FORMER FLOUR SACKS HAVE BEEN GIVEN NEW LIFE AND MADE INTO CUSHION COVERS AT VINTAGE BY NINA. OLD FRUIT SACKS HAVE BEEN HAND-STITCHED TO CREATE AN INFORMAL RUG. ON A 1950S ARMCHAIR UPHOLSTERED IN TICKING AND PLAIN LINEN SITS AN EMBROIDERED CUSHION BY HIP DANISH BRAND DAY BIRGER ET MIKKELSEN.

FINISHING TOUCHES

Cushions, throws and other accessories are vital as decorative punctuation marks in a living room. They could be very simple, in plain colours that contrast pleasantly with shades used elsewhere in the room – a chocolate brown woollen throw over a cream sofa arm, perhaps. Or they could be vibrant focal points, creating personality and drama. In an otherwise neutral room, for example, one Indian batik print used as a wall hanging or made into a bolster cover would lift the entire scheme. These small finishing touches are where it is possible to introduce colour, pattern and texture extravagantly, if you so wish. A blanket-stitched cashmere throw, an old flour sack with French monograms, a deep feather trim, a sequinned cushion cover – all wonderfully appealing and surprisingly easy to achieve.

It is relatively straightforward to make cushion covers, or inexpensive to have them made for you – at all costs, avoid cheap high-street scatter cushions that simply don't go with anything else. Almost any fabric can be employed, within reason. You could use remnants from a fabric that is used elsewhere in the room, or choose

BELOW A white embroidered cushion on a white sofa is effortlessly chic, accessorized by the dramatic textural contrast of a cashmere throw fringed with dyed feathers.

BELOW RIGHT An appealing window seat is piled with cushions of different sizes, shapes and styles, some new, some vintage. The throw has been made from a fabulous combination of linen and wool.

complementary patterns and colours in a completely different fabric. Or go to town with expensive fabrics, since you will need such a small amount – a square metre could easily make four square cushion fronts, using cheaper fabric for the back. Alternatively, use vintage fragments for a fashionably eclectic look. Even a favourite dress, duvet cover or tea towel/dishtowel could be cut, stitched and turned into something new. Floor cushions, screens, bolsters, wall hangings and fabric-covered storage boxes are only slightly more complex to make, using appealing fabrics and trims. The key is to keep an eye on the details as well as the bigger picture, to create an integrated scheme that looks effortless, inviting and interesting.

RIGHT In this room by interior designer Rose Uniacke, colour is subtle and texture reigns supreme. An armchair upholstered in suede is complemented by a simple linen-covered cushion.

BELOW RIGHT Studded leather floor cushions, ideal for low-level living, make eye-catching accessories in this room by Piet Boon.

PRACTICALITIES: CURTAIN LININGS

Lining is advised for all curtains except sheers, and can be useful for roman blinds, too. It helps fabric to hang neatly and protects it from fading, dirt and condensation. Usually made from a tightly woven fabric (cotton or poly-cotton), and available in a range of weights, it is generally white or cream, though coloured linings are also available. Thermal linings are coated on one side to reflect heat back into the room, and can be as effective as double glazing. Blackout lining has the same properties as thermal lining, but also blocks out light and, to a certain extent, noise. Inter-lining, as its name suggests, is sewn between the fabric and the lining to improve drape, body and heat retention. Linings may shrink at a different rate to curtains when washed, so either pre-wash, make them detachable or prepare to have the whole lot dry-cleaned.

STYLE TIPS

Perfectly matched chair and sofa covers, cushions, window treatments and accessories are unnecessary in a living room; instead, an individual mixture of plains/solids and subtle patterns is the way to go, incorporating a variety of appealing textures and trims.

ALL-NEUTRAL schemes can be gorgeous. To avoid monotony, incorporate highlights of one or two strong colours, textures or patterns – perhaps the edging on a throw, a lampshade or a couple of cushion covers.

PATTERNS, even very muted ones, help to disguise wear and tear on hard-working sofas. You can even combine different patterns within one slipcover to create an informal, boho look.

INEXPENSIVE fabrics are best used in generous amounts; make them up really well and use more luxurious fabrics to create borders, details and trims.

THE STYLE of a sofa cover can set the tone of a living room, whether formal, relaxed, cosy, elegant or quirky.

KITCHENS & DINING ROOMS

Since kitchens are full of hard surfaces, straight
lines and plain, mostly neutral colours, bringing
in lovely fabrics creates a welcome counterpoint
of warmth and softness, pattern and texture, and
introduces interesting touches that generally
brighten and add comfort to the space.

'Plain/solid colours that complement an understated modern kitchen or dining area look just as effective as country-style ginghams or florals in a more rustic space, or flamboyant patterns in a room where the intention is to create an impact.'

In kitchens and eating areas, it is more important than ever to choose the right fabric for function and location. This is not the most hospitable environment for delicate materials that require handling with care; unless you are decorating a formal dining room, you will need robust yarns that wash and wear well.

With regard to colour and pattern, however, the choice is virtually limitless. Plain/solid colours that complement an understated modern kitchen or dining area look just as effective as country-style ginghams or florals in a more rustic space, or flamboyant patterns in a room where the intention is to create an impact. Since these are highlights rather than an integral part of the structure of the room, you have the freedom to use them quite confidently, and of course to change them when you want to transform the character and feel of the room.

Fabrics make even more of a statement in a dining room than they do in a kitchen, contributing to the ambience of the space in the form of window treatments, seat covers, table dressings and accessories. A dining room without at least a few comfortable cushions, a pretty cloth or place mats on the table and an attractive curtain or blind would be a very dull place indeed.

WINDOW TREATMENTS

Kitchen window treatments usually have function as their first priority. They may be required for privacy or to hide a horrible view, to keep out draughts and keep in the warmth, or simply to make the room feel more cosy at night. And since it is common practice to position the kitchen sink in front of a window, many window treatments have specific requirements – they must not flap around or dangle into things, and they must be able to withstand the odd splash of water.

For these reasons, the most practical style of window treatment in a kitchen is often a blind: simple, neat, easy and inexpensive. Pull-down roller blinds fitted inside the window recess are ideal and, though rather plain, can be given a dash of interest in the form of an attractive trim or pull. Some also come with a cut-out bottom edge,

OPPOSITE When conventional cupboard doors are either too expensive or don't suit the style of your kitchen, a fabric curtain is a quick and easy way to screen off clutter. A white rectangle hemmed on all edges would take minutes to make, and can be tied up with a row of ribbons.

which gives them an additional element of sophistication. It may be useful, in certain situations, to make them with a translucent panel at the top to admit light, with an opaque section at the bottom for privacy. Alternatively, it is possible to find a type of roller blind which can be attached to the bottom of the window, to be pulled upwards to any height you wish.

Roman blinds tend to create a more sophisticated impression than most roller blinds, and could be made with a contrasting border or bottom edge. Roll-up blinds, as the name suggests, are lengths of hemmed fabric, suspended across the top of the window, that can be rolled up from the bottom and secured at any height by tying the rolled section with tapes or ribbons. Traditional in Sweden, roll-up blinds are a little more decorative than a straightforward roll-down roller blind, not only because of the pretty ties, but also because the reverse of the

blind is visible, offering the opportunity for an appealing combination of fabrics – perhaps two contrasting plains/solids, or a check and a floral.

In general, for the sake of practicality, it is a sensible idea (where possible) to fasten blinds to their wall attachments with hook-and-loop tape, so that they can be easily removed for cleaning.

Another option for a kitchen window which simply requires a little privacy is a sheer or very lightweight curtain. As a full-length or café (lower half only) curtain, this could be sewn with a header tape and hung in the usual way from a pole or track or, for simplicity, given a deep hem at the top and threaded over a bamboo rod or length of dowelling, or gathered onto a plastic-coated, stretchy wire, hung on small hooks at each end.

Ties, tabs, clips and eyelets are alternative hanging methods for light kitchen curtains, and you can use some

ABOVE For a country kitchen look, gathered gingham is ideal. In this utility room, it has been used as a curtain around the base of the sink.

OPPOSITE This appealingly understated roll-up blind has been made from a length of ticking lined with pale blue linen and tied with ribbon.

ingenuity when it comes to fabric: cotton, linen and polyester are all fine, but if you are prepared to improvise you could use found fabric such as a panel of antique lace, a couple of patterned tea towels/dishtowels stitched together or a small tablecloth – no need for hemming with either, while possible embellishments include embroidery, a ric rac or delicate crochet edging, beads or ribbons.

A quick word on another type of curtain that makes a charming addition to an informal, freestanding kitchen: a lightweight panel used instead of solid doors to screen base cupboards or the underneath of a sink. Often made from gingham, 1950s-style prints or tiny florals (because these really suit this plain, slightly retro look), such curtains are simply hung from a slim rod or stretchy cord, perhaps tightly gathered along an upper hem or attached with fabric ties.

In kitchens with larger windows which require a dressing that makes more of an impact – perhaps a set of French windows to the garden – or in most dining rooms, curtains can be more elaborate, providing an attractive background for cooking and eating. They may be softly gathered or pencil pleated and hung from a pole or track, or feature punched-metal eyelets and suspended from a tension wire – the options are really no different from those in a living room, and neither are the fabrics, though in general very heavy fabrics tend to look and feel odd in a kitchen, where the emphasis is not so much on a sumptuous appearance, and where they may suffer from the steam and smells of cooking.

OPPOSITE Dark-covered chairs are both practical and good-looking in a well-used dining room. The chic elegance of the chairs is tempered by the sheer prettiness of the Indian embroidered and mirrored fabric that has been made into curtains.

RIGHT Having found a dining chair she liked, Marijke van Nunen had a whole set made, with higher backs for comfort, and upholstered in beige linen to coordinate with full-length curtains.

SEAT COVERS & CUSHIONS

Seat covers can play a crucial role in a kitchen, whether they are intended to be used on mismatched chairs around an informal dining table, on stools at a breakfast bar or on a bench seat. Some kitchens are even large enough to accommodate a comfortable armchair or a small sofa pushed into a corner. Ginghams and chintzes tend to work well in country-style kitchens, while stripes and graphic patterns suit modern rooms and plains/solids work well pretty much anywhere. In a dining room with a set of high-backed chairs, seat covers are the sophisticated finishing touch that sets off the colour scheme, tableware and other elements. Coordinating, though not necessarily matching, table linen with curtains is a good idea, and plains/solids tend to be the

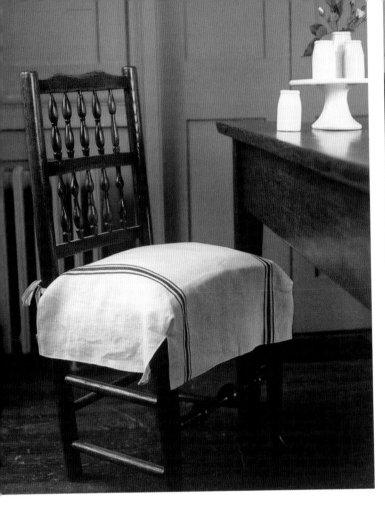

most popular choice, perhaps because they don't detract from the tasks of presenting and eating food. On the other hand, stripes are elegant and florals are pretty; and bolder patterns can work brilliantly in the right setting.

Whether seat covers are fixed or loose, the fabric that they are made from needs to be comfortable to sit on and neither too slippery nor too coarse. It should wear well and be of a suitable weight and texture for the piece that is covered. Tightly woven, medium- to heavyweight cottons, linens and blends are always a good choice, and if they are stain-resistant or behave well when washed, so much the better. A good retailer will provide essential information such as suitable washing temperatures and the results of wear tests.

For a sophisticated set of dining chairs or stools with matching fixed covers, leather (black or brown) is a popular choice. It is luxurious, hard-wearing and will wipe clean – within reason. Another upmarket option is

suede or, perhaps more practically, faux suede, which is actually made from polyester and is available at reasonable prices in a wide range of colours; what's more, it can be washed at home easily. It's always worth spending some time sitting on upholstered chairs before buying, to make sure that you don't slide off them and that the general shape, the upholstery padding and the fabric cover are really comfortable.

Slipcovers are the perfect option when the seating beneath them is badly mismatched, excessively worn or simply embarrassingly unattractive – or, of course, if you have young children and you know that it will be necessary to wash the covers regularly. Slipcovers can be very tight-fitting for the smartest look – made with piped/corded seams, box pleats or a scalloped or ruffled hem, for example. Alternatively, they can be casual and genuinely 'loose', with the simplest versions consisting of just a few rectangles of calico

ABOVE LONG CURTAINS ARE NOT ALWAYS POSSIBLE OR ADVISABLE IN A KITCHEN, BUT WHERE SPACE ALLOWS THEY CAN LOOK FABULOUS, AS DEMONSTRATED BY THIS PAIR OF FULL-LENGTH LINEN CURTAINS IN THE KITCHEN OF DUTCH DESIGNER PIET BOON.

ABOVE LEFT GRAB A CUSHION IF YOU NEED TO GET COMFORTABLE – THE OWNER OF THIS DINING ROOM HAS PILED UP A SET, ALL COVERED IN FABULOUS, DRAMATIC PATTERNS BY FLORENCE BROADHURST.

ABOVE Cushion covers can be finished in numerous ways; both simple and attractive is a set of ties, such as these on a linen cushion from Teed Interiors.

OPPOSITE Tie-on slipcovers are the easiest to make, and these use striped cotton from Ikea, which is both durable and washable. They coordinate with a neat set of roller blinds, pulling the scheme together in a way that looks far more expensive than it really is.

sewn together and pulled over the seat back, fastened with ties. Easily made, such covers can be changed with the seasons or even to suit the occasion.

Of course, the comfort of any type of dining chair, stool or bench is vital, and sometimes it's not a cover that is needed but just a cushion or two, whether for seats alone, or for both seats and backs. For practicality's sake, they should be well enough padded to provide pleasant support, but not so squashy that the sitter slips off them. Naturally, they should be a good fit for the seating – just the right width and depth so they don't buckle or move around. And they should look good. Much like slipcovers, they can be used to unify a group of otherwise disparate chairs and, if you choose interesting fabric, they can even become a focal point of the decorative scheme.

Cushions can range in style from the straightforward – two squares sewn together – to the elaborate, featuring deep ruffles, contrast piping/cording, envelope backs or button fastenings. Box cushions tend to be comfortable to sit on, and ties are useful for keeping them in place. Most types of fabric, within reason, can be used (as long as they are neither very heavy nor light, slippery or overly textured). Offcuts from larger projects are ideal, as are the good bits from otherwise-worn sheets, duvet covers, tablecloths or even clothing. Tea towels/dishtowels are ideal, as are canvas, chambray and other hard-wearing natural fabrics; or you could opt for something more classy – you need such small quantities that even expensive new fabric won't cost the earth. Simply think about what best suits the look of the room as a whole.

THIS PAGE OLD FRENCH MONOGRAMMED NAPKINS, FROM VINTAGE BY NINA, CREATE A SIMPLE BUT SOPHISTICATED TABLE SETTING WHEN COMBINED WITH PLAIN WHITE CHINA, DISTRESSED WOOD AND LARGE FLOWER HEADS.

RIGHT AND ABOVE BOX-SHAPED SEAT
CUSHIONS CAN BE EXTREMELY COMFORTABLE;
THESE ARE MADE FROM A FLORAL FABRIC FROM
VINTAGE BY NINA. THEY LOOK PARTICULARLY
AT HOME IN THE CORNER OF THIS COUNTRY
KITCHEN, WITH ITS TONGUE-AND-GROOVE WALLS,
WHITE PAINTWORK AND WIREWORK BASKETS.

DRESSING THE TABLE

Whether you prefer to eat in the kitchen or a separate
dining room, there will be occasions, perhaps regularly,
perhaps only now and then, when you will want to
dress the table. Also, more generally, tables need to be
protected from any damage from hot plates and dishes,
or from the wet bases of mugs, cups and glasses. For
this purpose, your best friends are place mats and
coasters. They could be made from quilted cotton or
linen, tough denim (it comes in plenty of colours other
than blue), thick felt or even, if you are handy with a
needle, crocheted cotton, raffia or leather thong. If you
are making rectangles or squares of fabric, you can use
all sorts of remnants, old or new, and embellish them
in a variety of ways to suit your style, including ric rac
or ribbon, embroidery or appliqué.

LEFT Bold splashes of colour create a fresh, vibrant feel in this open-plan living and dining area, which harmoniously combines Scandinavian and Italian design influences. In what is essentially a simple scheme, white walls and plain, white modern furnishings form the backdrop for brightly patterned cushions and a tablecloth by the Finnish design company Marimekko. The black-and-white china on the table is by Missoni Home of Italy.

BELOW ECRU NAPKINS WITH NARROW NAUTICAL STRIPES SET AGAINST BROWN LINEN TABLE MATS ARE THE HEIGHT OF SEASIDE CHIC.

BELOW RIGHT A SENSE OF CLASSIC DESIGN COMBINED WITH MODERN WIT AND STYLE PERVADES THIS SLEEK DINING ROOM BY JOB INTERIEUR. THE TABLE IS DRESSED WITH WHITE LINEN RUNNERS, COMPLEMENTED BY A PAIR OF OVERSIZED CLEAR-GLASS CANDLE-HOLDERS.

For young children's mealtimes and to protect an all-purpose kitchen table against potential damage from painting or craft activities, a wipe-clean, plastic-coated oilcloth is invaluable. These frequently come in jolly checks or vivid flower patterns which brighten up any room. For general mealtimes, a cotton or linen cloth in a light to medium weight is ideal; for obvious reasons, avoid loose, textured or pile weaves. If you don't like ironing, it is wise to steer clear of pure linen since it creases easily (just like those summer trousers) and choose a linen blend instead. Sheets (non-synthetic, please) make ideal tablecloths, come ready hemmed and are often less expensive than buying fabric by the metre.

To create a particular look, and when necessary a sense of occasion, you can go to town with table dressings. For a formal setting, nothing beats a beautiful antique cloth in lace or damask, perhaps with a crocheted edge or embroidered motifs. You could layer two differently sized cloths, contrasting their colours and textures – especially effective when the top one is lace. Shaped or ruffled borders in the same or a contrast fabric add interest or, for a rustic look, you could make a large, patchwork-effect tablecloth out of four smaller squares of coordinating fabric, or cut oversized flower shapes from a gingham or floral fabric and appliqué them onto a plain background.

Table runners – long, narrow strips of fabric which 'run' along the length of a dining table – are the alternative to a cloth when creating an elegant atmosphere. Since you are not putting plates on them, you can afford to be

ABOVE IN WHAT MIGHT OTHERWISE BE A VERY CLINICAL ROOM, WITH ITS COMBINATION OF STAINLESS STEEL AND HIGH-GLOSS WHITE WORK SURFACES, THE CRISP LINEN TABLECLOTH AND FRESHLY LAUNDERED NAPKINS INTRODUCE A SOFTER, MORE HOMELY FEEL.

ABOVE LEFT USING SLIM MOTHER-OF-PEARL BANDS IN PLACE OF CONVENTIONAL NAPKIN RINGS CREATES A VISUAL LINK BETWEEN THE THICK, LUXURIOUS NAPKINS AND THE UNADORNED WOODEN TABLE.

OPPOSITE Natural fabrics bring comfort and simplicity to this utilitarian dining area. Linen and velvet cushions soften the metal chairs, while raw silk place mats and velvet-trimmed linen napkins are casually laid on an old French linen sheet, which is used as a tablecloth.

ABOVE These ribbon and button fastenings add a colourful finishing touch to a set of rolled-up napkins.

ABOVE CENTRE A well-laundered linen sheet makes a fresh and attractive tablecloth. The lace panel that has been hung at the window is by Anna French.

ABOVE RIGHT Remnants of cotton or linen, perhaps trimmed with ribbon or velvet, make ideal napkins. If they don't match perfectly, it really doesn't matter.

a little more adventurous with the fabric, which could be thinner, thicker or more textured than a conventional cloth. A loose weave such as hessian, a light fabric such as organza or a heavy fabric such as tweed could all, potentially, look great. Pointed ends, fringes, tassels, beading, contrast borders and other embellishments are further possibilities.

ACCESSORIES & FINISHING TOUCHES

The finishing touch for a well-laid table is often a set of napkins. They could be plain/solid or patterned, perhaps made from inexpensive cotton gingham, a pretty floral or antique monogrammed linen, or other variations of plain/solid or patterned, medium-weight natural fabrics which wash and wear well. Add a trim of velvet ribbon, blanket-stitch edging or a naive embroidered motif if you wish to make them more decorative. Even napkin 'rings' made from ribbons, ric rac, lace or bias-bound strips of offcut fabrics, fastened with beautiful buttons, can be employed to enhance the overall effect.

Other small fabric accessories, generally for kitchen rather than dining-room use, could include such practical but pretty things as tray cloths, linings for storage boxes, hand towels, oven gloves, aprons and tea cosies. These can sometimes create a focal point or set a style that is taken up elsewhere – a vintage-lace cake cover, for example, could be complemented with a lace-edged tablecloth or a set of cushions.

For kitchens with a laundry area, meanwhile, there are accessories such as ironing-board covers, peg tidies and drawstring linen bags – doing the laundry is less of a chore when you can surround yourself with beautiful things that make you feel better about it. All these items can easily be made at home from scraps of new or vintage fabrics, perhaps embroidered, patched or trimmed in an interesting way (though not embellished to the extent that they become unusable). The trick is, however, for all these small items to work together. If each is made from a different, completely unrelated fabric remnant, the effect will be messy. Though these are tiny details, they add greatly to the overall look, so aim to coordinate colours and patterns, echoing the style of the room and of the fabrics used for curtains, table linen and seat covers, and the result will be as delightfully good-looking as it is functional.

BELOW LEFT A WIDE RANGE OF KITCHEN ACCESSORIES CAN BE STORED CONVENIENTLY IN FABRIC-LINED BOXES.

BELOW CENTRE THERE ARE KITSCH TEA COSIES AND – LESS FREQUENTLY – THERE ARE SOPHISTICATED TEA COSIES. THIS ONE, BY DAY BIRGER ET MIKKELSEN, DEFINITELY FALLS INTO THE LATTER CATEGORY.

BELOW RIBBON TRIMS ADD INTEREST TO THE SIMPLEST OF NAPKINS.

OPPOSITE THE DELICACY OF THIS VINTAGE-LACE FOOD COVER FROM VINTAGE BY NINA IS ABSOLUTELY GORGEOUS – WELL SUITED TO A DISPLAY ON A DINING TABLE OR KITCHEN SHELVES, EVEN WITHOUT A CAKE BENEATH IT.

BELOW FABRICS FREQUENTLY COMBINE THE TWO ATTRIBUTES OF BEAUTY AND USEFULNESS, AS EXEMPLIFIED BY THIS APRON MADE FROM A COMBINATION OF LINEN AND TICKING.

BELOW RIGHT NO NEED FOR PLASTIC BAGS – THIS ROOMY, HARD-WORKING SHOPPER HAS BEEN MADE FROM OLD FRUIT SACKS.

PRACTICALITIES: KEEPING FABRICS CLEAN AND FRESH

Have you spilt red wine, gravy or greasy sauce on a white tablecloth? Tomato ketchup on a linen napkin? Orange juice on a tea towel/dishtowel? There is no need to worry – most stains on fabrics can be removed successfully with a little care and knowhow.

The most important thing to bear in mind is that the longer a stain is left untackled, the more difficult it is to get out. Prompt attention is always best (unless the fabric label specifies that the item must be dry-cleaned – in which case, do nothing but take it to the cleaners as soon as possible). And remember to work at the stain from the inside out, thereby pushing the

RIGHT Since tea towels/dishtowels are so inexpensive, it's worth choosing a few that make an impact, whether with a classic red-on-white stripe, as in this kitchen, or a more contemporary pattern.

BELOW Scraps of vintage floral and gingham fabric have been used to make these pretty napkins.

staining substance away from the fabric, rather than further into it. For liquid stains, blot up as much as possible, using a clean, white cloth. Dab gently – hard rubbing will simply push the stain further into the fabric. Then, if the stain is still visible, try a gentle dab with cool water and blot again. Thicker substances, such as paint, nail varnish or mud, should be scraped away with a smooth-bladed knife, while greasy residues may be absorbed with a sprinkling of talcum powder.

Stubborn stains can usually be removed by the application of a proprietary treatment, available from any store selling household cleaners, but if you prefer to avoid these harsh chemicals, water-based stains may be treated with bicarbonate of soda or white vinegar, while protein-based stains (blood, egg, milk and so on) may be tackled with biological detergent.

STYLE TIPS

Introduce colour, pattern and a little softness into a kitchen (which may otherwise be full of rather hard and linear furnishings) by using fabric accessories. In a dining room, curtains and table linen will create an individual ambience.

A CRISP white tablecloth looks smart whatever the occasion and can hide the plainest of tables. If you decide to use patterned cloth, aim to coordinate with your china and other elements in the room.

LOOSELY fitted seat covers made from white or off-white cotton or linen will disguise ugly chairs and unify mismatching sets. Just put them in the washing machine when necessary.

VINTAGE napkins, runners, tea towels/dishtowels or cushion covers have a homely, welcoming appeal. Pick them up at car-boot sales/garage sales, in junk shops or from craft fairs – if you choose colours and patterns carefully, you can create a harmonious assortment that conveys a stylishly informal effect.

BLINDS are best kept as simple as possible, though a pretty trim or pull adds interest. For dining-room windows, however, you might wish for a grander set of curtains in a luxurious fabric.

BEDROOMS

Nowhere do we get as intimate with fabrics as in the bedroom, and this is a room in which, once the practicalities have been satisfied, pure indulgence can be allowed free rein, with luxury and comfort becoming your main concerns.

'Whites and off-whites, pale colours, small checks and narrow stripes all make a good foundation for a sophisticated bedroom scheme, with touches of darker, bolder colours, or a dash of eye-catching pattern, for dramatic interest.'

Details count when it comes to choosing fabrics for the bedroom: the intricate edging around a plain white duvet cover, the piping/cording on a delicate chair, the frill around a pretty cushion. But the big picture is important, too: combining plains/solids with patterns or modern with vintage, layering texture on texture – to put together a serene and luxurious, utterly alluring personal retreat.

Decorating a bedroom is a wonderful opportunity to create a private space – a space in which you can feel completely at ease, with no need to worry about anyone else's requirements. As long as it has a comfortable bed and efficient storage, a bedroom has no great functional specifications. It should provide enough floor area for easy dressing, a convenient mirror and somewhere for you to brush your hair and put on make-up. Beyond that, it is all about indulgence, relaxation, and making sure the environment is conducive to getting a good night's sleep. How you use fabrics, therefore, is vital. Their colours, patterns and textures will complement the hard surfaces and straight lines of the bed, wardrobe and chests of drawers, draw the eye as focal points within the room and contribute to pleasant acoustics, tactile surfaces and an overall sense of warmth and well-being.

Although the atmosphere of a bedroom should be soft and inviting, it is not obligatory to use fabrics in a flouncy, fussy way. In fact, the key to getting bedroom fabrics right is to keep things simple. Comfortable bed linen and effective window treatments are the necessities, and in many cases the plainer the better, since vivid colours and bold patterns are best avoided in a room which should feel tranquil and calm.

Whites and off-whites, pale colours, small checks and narrow stripes all make a good foundation for a sophisticated bedroom scheme, with touches of darker, bolder colours, or a dash of eye-catching pattern, for drama. Subtle interest can come in the form of self-coloured damask and jacquard weaves, embroidery and edgings. Texture plays an important role, too; think of combinations such as linen and velvet, satin and mohair, lambswool and fleece. A little luxury can go a long way.

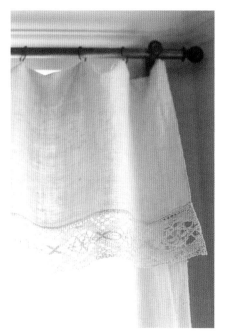

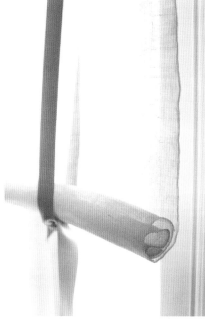

LEFT THIS ROLL-UP BLIND IS MADE FROM
RAMIE, THE FIBRE FROM A SHRUBBY PLANT.
THE FABRIC IS BY CMO AT TAPET-CAFÉ.

FAR LEFT IN A FEMININE BEDROOM, A LACE-
EDGED PELMET/VALANCE OVER A LINEN CURTAIN
IS PRETTY WITHOUT BEING FUSSY.

OPPOSITE IN THIS LUXURIOUS BEDROOM BY
ROSE UNIACKE, OVER-LONG CURTAINS MADE
FROM LINEN DRAPE ELEGANTLY ON THE FLOOR.

WINDOW TREATMENTS

The days of carefully matched bed linen and window treatments are long
past (thankfully, many people would say) and yet it is important to get this
pairing right. When the bed is plain, some pattern at the window is lovely,
and vice versa. What you should avoid is two patterns which clash. And it is
effective to echo a detail of one in the other – the colour of a curtain in a
trim on a bedspread, for example.

Plain curtains can look beautiful if made from a generous amount of fabric
with deep gathers, perhaps even draping a little onto the floor. They may be
hung from a pole with pretty finials at the ends – glass teardrops, perhaps, or
a carved wooden sphere – and finished with an edging of ruffles, a contrast
border or rows of wide ribbons, or with a lacy pelmet/valance across the top.
If lack of privacy is a problem, it may be necessary to add sheer or lace
curtains, either full-length or covering the bottom half of the window only.

Depending on how badly your sleep is disturbed by early morning light, a
blackout lining may be an essential addition to your bedroom curtains. This
also helps to retain heat, but if heat loss is a real issue (hands up anyone

THIS PAGE Two long colour-coordinated ribbons are used to tie up this blind, made in a fabric from Malabar. The embroidered bed linen is by Designers Guild and the bedspread is by Day Birger et Mikkelsen.

ABOVE AND RIGHT Diaphanous white sheers, billowing gently in the breeze, are the perfect window treatment for a bedroom overlooking the ocean. In this Danish seaside home, they reinforce the blue-and-white nautical theme.

with beautiful but draughty old sash windows) it is also worth adding a thermal lining. You could simply layer two fabrics together, or use a length of fleece, felt or similarly dense but soft material as an effective improvisation.

Blinds may seem too understated for a bedroom, but in fact they can be extremely elegant, and there are different options to suit different styles of room. A roller blind in a neutral colour will blend into the background

in a contemporary minimalist space or, in a more formal room, could be used in conjunction with 'dress' curtains (attached either side of the window). Roman blinds pull up in lovely soft folds that give an attractive drape without looking too elaborate, while roll-up blinds – which are literally rolled up from the bottom and tied in position – show off their reverse, thereby offering an attractive combination of two fabrics.

As for fabric for curtains and blinds, there are practical limits in terms of not using anything too heavy or too flimsy but, within these limits, almost anything can work. Cottons, linens, wools and their blends, in various weights from denim to organza, are all ideal, and there is a wealth of alternatives to conventional weaves and finishes, from men's suiting to devoré velvet. Be open to less conventional choices, too, whether hemp, paper, mohair, denim or fleece, or found options such as saris, blankets, quilts or tablecloths.

The way in which curtains are hung is crucial to their final look. It could be from a header with pleats or gathers in various widths and styles, or by means of ties, tabs, eyelets or clips. Generally, the less full the gathers the more modern the end result. Poles or tracks are best attached so that they extend far enough each side of the window to allow you to pull the curtains right back, letting as much light into the room as possible during the day. And if you can't stand

LEFT CHOCOLATE BROWN, BEIGE AND WHITE
COMBINE TO CREATE A RESTFUL ROOM FULL
OF TEXTURE AND INTEREST, THANKS TO AN
ECLECTIC SELECTION OF ACCESSORIES FOUND
BY THE OWNERS ON THEIR TRAVELS. THE SHELL
FRINGING ON THE LINEN LAMPSHADE AND THE
SEQUINS ON THE CUSHIONS AND BEDSPREAD
ADD SUBTLE TOUCHES OF GLAMOUR; THE FRAMED
LENGTH OF FABRIC ON THE WALL ABOVE THE BED
GIVES THE IMPRESSION OF A HEADBOARD.

the look of a bare track or plain pole, a pelmet/valance is the answer, which can also help play visual tricks with proportions: hung high above a window, a pelmet/valance can make the window seem taller; if hung low, it has the opposite effect. Normally made from wood or MDF/composite board to about one-sixth of the depth of the curtain, and either rectangular in shape or scrolling, solid pelmets/valances can either be painted or covered in a fabric to match or coordinate with your curtains. So that the fabric can be removed for cleaning, it is advisable to mount it on a stiffened backing, then attach it to the pelmet with hook-and-loop tape.

BED TREATMENTS

The rise of the duvet has meant, sadly, that we now rarely make our beds with traditional flat sheets topped with old-fashioned blankets, quilts and eiderdowns. With a combination of well-chosen bed linens, however, it is still possible to create the comfortable feel and appealing look that result from layers of contrasting textures, colours and patterns.

First, the basics: sheets, pillowcases and duvet covers. Since we spend about a third of our lives in bed, it is worth investing in quality; if made from high-quality fabrics, these essentials will not only feel more comfortable next to the skin but they will also wash well and last for years. All but the most

ABOVE AND ABOVE RIGHT These pillowcases were made from old Belgian flour sacks. The bedhead is an ikat-dyed cashmere hung from a slim pole. The bedding is a luxurious combination of linen, velvet and cashmere.

OPPOSITE Careful combining of diverse colours, patterns and styles can result in an interesting and appealing look. The quilt is from Toast and the embroidered bed linen from Designers Guild. The padded headboard was made using fabric from Zoffany and the curtains were adapted from cutwork Indian bedspreads from The Cloth Shop.

basic duvet covers and pillows are likely to offer interesting design details, from pintucks, piping/cording and scalloped edging to hemstitch, embroidery and lace – not to mention choice of colours and printed patterns. But before you even reach this stage, the big question is which fibre to choose. Any linen enthusiast will tell you that nothing can beat pure linen. It has excellent breathability, a cool, crisp touch and becomes softer as it gets older – but it does require ironing. Silk also has its fans. It too is highly breathable, keeping you warm in winter and cool in summer; it's even said to reduce wrinkles and keep your hair glossy. Silk needs gentle handling but it can go in the washing machine. Cotton, though, is by far the most popular choice; pure Egyptian cotton is generally considered the finest in the world. Look for a thread count (closeness of the weave) of more than 200, and up to 600 for real luxury.

scrolling headboard with carved detailing
is a French antique padded with vintage
floral fabric. The quilt is made from silk,
with patterned stitching, and the cushion
cover is another vintage floral fabric.
The reds and pinks, though in different
patterns, work effectively together.

Cotton is not just cotton, however; it can come in the form of percale, satin, sateen, waffle, jacquard, flannel, jersey and corduroy, each with a different feel and style. There is also easy-care, a 50:50 mix of cotton and polyester, which has obvious advantages.

The quickest and easiest way to put together a gorgeous-looking bed is to use plain white or off-white sheets, pillow cases and duvet cover, and add one stunning bedcover. This could be a throw, blanket, eiderdown or quilt, modern or vintage, subtle and chic or charmingly rustic. These days, high-street stores have a fantastic selection of striking bed linens, while a little hunting around sale rooms, second-hand shops, the internet or even car-boot/garage sales may well result in some superb finds.

Buy why stop at just one layer? If you wish, add another bedcover and a few throws and start experimenting with different combinations, some spread out over the bed, some folded and others hung artfully over the foot. An eiderdown and a quilt, one a large-scale floral and the other a small, spriggy one, in similar colours, could look very effective together, for example, as would a couple of dark throws folded on the end of a bed that has been made up with stark white linens. Select luscious textures (crochet, tweed, angora, say) and interesting trims (satin ribbon, blanket stitch, cutwork embroidery) and you won't go far wrong.

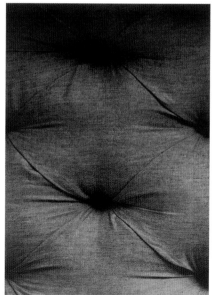

ABOVE AND ABOVE CENTRE A clever idea
from Piet Boon: this deeply buttoned
headboard is luxury enough, but when
given enclosing wings it is reminiscent of
chairs in a gentlemen's club, while also
being stylish, witty and pleasingly cosy.

ABOVE RIGHT Another take on the
oversized, buttoned headboard is this
sophisticated example by JOB Interieur.

OPPOSITE It pays to use a range of
sumptuous textures in a bedroom. This
room by Atelier Abigail Ahern includes a
crocheted bedspread (with a fabulously
huge pattern repeat) and cushions made
from felt and knitted wool.

HEADBOARDS

The great advantage of styling a bed by creating layers is that it can all easily
be changed, almost in an instant. Headboards, however, tend to be more
permanent fixtures – though there is always the possibility of making
slipcovers for summer and winter. The fabric for a headboard should work
well with everything else in the room, from bed linen to walls and window
treatments, and, though it needn't be exceptionally durable, shouldn't be too
fragile, either. Lusciously soft and tactile fabrics are a particularly satisfying
choice – think of velvet, moleskin or lambswool, for example. If headboards
are deeply padded (and maybe buttoned too), it makes them more
comfortable to lean on, and for real opulence you could even have a winged
headboard made that wraps right around the top of the bed.

Using a fabric-covered screen is an easier alternative that will create
approximately the same effect. Or you could simply throw a quilt over the
bedhead, or make a rectangle of quilted fabric that ties onto the metal
framework. For divan beds, a rectangular headboard can either be attached
to the wall or to the bed frame, padded with a sheet of wadding and then
covered with the fabric of your choice.

CHAIRS AND SIDE TABLES

Not many bedrooms are large enough to accommodate a full-sized sofa, but there is sometimes space for a small sofa or chaise longue, a pretty armchair, a dressing-table chair or maybe a stool. For upholstery or slipcovers, seat pads or scatter cushions, use fabrics that complement either the curtains or bed linen. If too many elements in a room are deliberately made to match, the scheme could end up looking twee, but coordinating colours and motifs in an unfussy way is always worthwhile.

Depending on the degree to which the fabrics are subjected to wear and tear (probably not much), you can afford to choose more delicate fabrics in a bedroom than elsewhere in the house, perhaps even ones that are dry-clean only. This could also provide an opportunity to experiment with antique and ethnic fabrics or, if you prefer to keep things simple, to enjoy the unassuming beauty of plain, even utilitarian, fabrics.

ABOVE BOLDLY CONTRASTED COLOURS AND TEXTURES ALWAYS ADD INTEREST: HERE, A WHITE LEATHER CHAIR IS SET AGAINST A NUBBLY BLACK SEAGRASS RUNNER BY PIET BOON.

LEFT THE SQUARE LINES OF A PLAIN WHITE DAYBED ARE A FOIL FOR PATCHWORK CUSHIONS MADE FROM VIBRANTLY STRIPED THAI SILKS.

FAR LEFT THIS UNUSUAL SIDE TABLE IS MADE FROM WIDE LENGTHS OF DYED AND WOVEN GRASS FABRIC. THE BROAD-STRIPED CURTAINS ARE IN SILK TAFFETA.

OPPOSITE THIS DARK AND HEAVY ARMCHAIR HAS BEEN TRANSFORMED BY A FRESH, PALE COVER AND COORDINATING CUSHION IN FABRIC BY SASHA WADDELL FOR TEED INTERIORS.

STORAGE

A great deal of space is taken up in most bedrooms by storage furniture: wardrobes, chests of drawers, tallboys, trunks, boxes and so on. These pieces can be good to look at in themselves, but if they are not as attractive as they might be, fabric could be the answer. To hide a cheap and cheerful hanging rail or wardrobe, for example, what could be easier than attaching a curtain across one side of the room, effectively sectioning it off as a dressing area? If the curtain matches those at the window, the scheme will look well thought out. Covering a shop-bought wooden or cane screen (or even one you have made yourself) with fabric has a similar effect. With some furniture, it is possible to remove the door panels and replace them with fabric, either stretched or ruched, depending on how contemporary or country you want it to look. Don't try this on proper antique furniture, however – you'll detract from its value. To disguise a truly dreadful piece of furniture, or even just to convey an extra element of softness and comfort, it is even possible to upholster certain pieces, much as you would a sofa or chair.

Boxes large and small offer additional storage solutions in a bedroom, whether pushed under a bed or on display. Linings (perhaps padded) or covers made from fabric will transform more or less any type of box. This is a great opportunity to use remnants from curtains or bedcovers and thereby pull the decorative scheme together. Small scraps of interesting fabric can also be used for coat hangers, lavender pouches and hanging decorations.

OPPOSITE To disguise a wall of clothes storage, the owner of this house has made a simple curtain which easily pulls right across whenever necessary. This is a cheap solution that fits the informality of the room, but it's worth investing in a good-quality fabric and ensuring that the curtains are really well made. The sequinned blankets are from a selection at Day Birger et Mikkelsen.

CHILDREN'S BEDROOMS

Children's rooms are always best designed with flexibility in mind. What's right for a baby won't suit a four-year-old, and a 12-year-old is, of course, another proposition entirely. The solution, if you don't want to spend a fortune updating the room every few years, is to keep the largest areas (walls, floors, sofa covers and so on) subtle in colour so that they stand the test of time, while smaller, less expensive items such as blinds, cushions, bedcovers and lampshades can be changed when necessary.

A baby's room can be really quite minimal. A peaceful atmosphere may be created with calm colours and patterns, and soft textures are, naturally, pre-eminent. Unfussy window treatments with blackout linings are ideal, and a simple set of cot/crib linen might consist of nothing more than white cotton sheets and a cosy fleece or cellular blanket with a satin trim, plus a quilted 'bumper' tied securely around the head of the cot/crib. You may be tempted to splash out on accessories – there are certainly enough in the shops – but there's really no need; it is better to wait until your children are a little older and you (and they) have a clearer idea of their personality and preferences.

When a child moves from a cot/crib to a bed, it usually signals a rethink of the entire room, and this is where colour and pattern take on greater significance, particularly when, as is often the case, your child has decided that she or he is a little ballerina or a princess, a knight or a cowboy.

In children's bedrooms, it can be tempting to follow convention and opt for bright colours and bold patterns, but there is no need to choose retina-aching

ABOVE Two matching pairs of cushions, covered in gingham and ticking, are adaptable and attractive accessories for a child's bedroom. Although pattern has been kept to a minimum and the colour scheme is limited to red, white and blue, the effect is cheerful and welcoming.

OPPOSITE Saris and other ethnic fabrics can be used to make flamboyant drapes above a child's bed. The chinoiserie-style cushion covers recall exotic lands.

Tre små engle skal følge dig,
på livets vej herned.
Den ene tro.
Den anden håb.
Den tredje kærlighed.

OPPOSITE Simplicity can be utterly beautiful in itself — especially when contrasted with the over-exuberance that sometimes characterizes a child's room. Here, a vintage quilt in subtle colours and a plain linen blind provide a quiet backdrop for either playing or sleeping.

RIGHT Adult patterns are fine for children's rooms — there really is no need to opt for cartoon characters or garish colours. Here, bold florals are complemented by the graphic blocks of a hand-made American patchwork quilt.

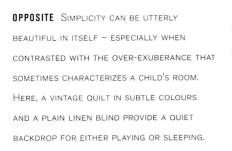

primaries that are utterly bereft of sophistication. A room full of neutrals might be too plain, but in a boy's room, for example, why not combine navy with highlights of lime green, or brown with touches of orange? And in a girl's room, why not mix some greys with the inevitable pink, or a shot of deep crimson with lilac? As for pattern, it is possible to be just as inventive in a child's bedroom as anywhere else. Don't restrict your search to so-called children's fabric only; many 'adult' fabrics work beautifully in a child's room, and may well be less expensive. While toiles, damasks and similarly traditional patterns will look out of place, checks are always charming, and there are plenty of really pretty floral, figurative, retro and ethnic patterns that are absolutely ideal.

As with any other room, patterns in a child's bedroom require careful coordination, and are often best used in

ABOVE IN AN ECHO OF THE COLOURFUL COLLAGES THAT DECORATE THE WALLS, THIS DAYBED IS FILLED WITH A COLLECTION OF FLORAL AND STRIPED CUSHIONS AND PRETTY BLANKETS MADE FROM CROCHET AND WELSH WOOL. BUNTING IS ANOTHER CHARMING ADDITION TO A CHILD'S ROOM, AND CAN EASILY BE MADE FROM SCRAPS OF FABRIC, TAILORED IN COLOUR AND PATTERN TO YOUR CHILD'S TASTE.

ABOVE RIGHT THIS GLORIOUS COMBINATION OF COLOURS IS OFF-BEAT BUT APPEALING. THE SILK BOLSTER WITH AN EXTRAVAGANT TASSEL (PERHAPS BEST RESERVED FOR AN OLDER CHILD) IS BY MARIJKE VAN NUNEN.

conjunction with plains/solids. For example, you could team a pair of long, plain curtains with a duvet cover in a pattern that includes a complementary colour; or give a plain/solid blind and bedcover trims cut from the same patterned fabric. Chair and sofa covers could be made from plain/solid fabric accompanied by patterned cushions, or you could make a slipcover from a patchwork of delightful remnants.

As in an adult's bedroom, you can layer quilts, throws, bedcovers and blankets – the result can be an enchanting jumble of colours, patterns and textures that is appealing to both adults and children. It goes without saying that fabrics in this room should be relatively tough, and that anything that might need cleaning would be best made from washable fabric.

A really lovely way to use fabrics in a child's room – more so, probably, than any other – is for charming accessories, particularly if you are good

with a sewing machine or needle. These might include squashy beanbags and floor cushions (made of jumbo cord, cotton velvet, denim, flannel or some other hard-wearing but comfortable fabric), or a mini tepee in which the kids can hide out. Sheer fabric drapes can be hung from the ceiling to create a princess bed, or appliquéd canopies hooked around a bunk bed to transform it into a castle, train, jungle camp or anywhere else your imagination takes you. For storage, you can make drawstring bags to hang at an easily accessible height around the walls, lined baskets and back-of-the-door tidies with multiple pockets. Even the smallest accessories, in pretty fabrics that coordinate with the room as a whole – whether strings of bunting made from multicoloured remnants or fabric-covered photograph frames or noticeboards – will help to pull the room together and create an ambience that's fun, functional and easy on the eye, for young and old alike.

ABOVE Truly girly, but not at all twee, the luscious colours and intricate pattern of this quilt, from Zara Home, are echoed in the party shoes.

ABOVE LEFT All girls seem to love pink, but the shade of the quilt in Piet Boon's daughter's room is far from the usual sugary or bubblegum colour. The vibrant fuschia, combined with muted green, is chic at the same time as being pretty.

PRACTICALITIES: LOOKING AFTER YOUR BED LINEN

Keep your bed comfortable and make your sheets, pillowcases and duvet covers last longer by treating them with a little loving care. It is advisable to wash new bed linen before using it, since manufacturers often treat fabrics with a finish that may irritate bare skin. Before washing, always check the label. Special fabrics should be dry-cleaned or washed by hand, as advised. Otherwise, divide loads for the machine into whites and coloureds, and by types of fabric, and wash accordingly. Keep whites bright by washing them separately and – where possible – line-drying in the sun. High-temperature washes are still necessary for heavily soiled loads, but it's possible to wash most bed linen at 30°C – new machines and detergents are more than able

RIGHT THIS CHILD'S ROOM BY MARIJKE VAN NUNEN FEATURES A SPACE-SAVING SECRET BED WITH EXCITING FABRICS: A PURPLE QUILT MADE FROM SILK AND PILES OF CRIMSON AND PATTERNED CUSHIONS.

to get good results while saving energy (about 40 per cent compared to a 40°C cycle). After washing and drying, fold and store, perhaps with a scented sachet tucked inside. If you have beds of different sizes, it's useful to label your linens so you know which goes where. A hand-embroidered monogram is one way to do this, but a dot from a permanent marker in a hidden corner would do the trick just as well. To lengthen the life of your mattress and pillows, use fitted protectors and, for additional comfort and support, add a mattress topper. Every day when you get up, throw back the bedclothes to air the bed for 20 minutes or so, then plump your pillows and fluff up the duvet. Airing the duvet outside (though not in direct sunlight) every now and then will help keep it really fresh, and to keep your mattress at its best, turn it over regularly and vacuum from time to time to remove fluff and dust.

STYLE TIPS

Personalize your bedroom by using gorgeous fabrics, the softer and more luxurious the better, to make you feel truly comfortable. Patterns and colours are best kept muted, but layering and luscious textures are the way to go.

CURTAINS AND BED LINEN cover large areas in a bedroom; you can avoid clashes by keeping either curtains or the bedcover relatively plain, and coordinating colours well.

BLACKOUT LININGS are invaluable for bedroom curtains and blinds. Consider having two sets – one in a dark, heavy fabric for winter and the other lighter and paler for summer. The same goes for any slipcovers.

LAYER bedclothes for a sumptuous effect. Start with sheets and blankets (or a duvet) and add an eiderdown, quilt, cover, throw, shawl or whatever else takes your fancy.

A CHILD'S BEDROOM need not be the space that taste forgot. Unexpected colours, interesting patterns and a range of charming accessories, in practical fabrics, all receive high marks for delivering both fun and function.

BATHROOMS

Nowhere is it more essential for fabrics to be both useful and beautiful than in a bathroom. From towels to window treatments, from drawstring bags to dressing gowns, they serve an essential purpose, but they also contribute enormously to the look and – importantly – the feel of the room.

'Bathrooms are, by necessity, furnished with ceramics and other cold, hard, shiny materials – and fabrics, although they don't play a lavish part, provide a balancing softness and warmth.'

OPPOSITE, LEFT THIS LUXURIOUS BATHROOM DESIGNED BY PIET BOON FEATURES CRISP, CLEAN LINES AND SUBTLE, NEUTRAL COLOURS. FLUFFY ROBES AND PILES OF FOLDED TOWELS COORDINATE IN COLOUR WITH THE ROUND BATH.

OPPOSITE, CENTRE PADDED UPHOLSTERY IS NOT ADVISABLE IN A STEAMY BATHROOM, BUT IF MOISTURE ISN'T AN ISSUE, THEN A DRAMATIC PIECE SUCH AS THIS BUTTONED ARMCHAIR BY JOB INTERIEUR CAN LOOK FANTASTIC.

OPPOSITE, RIGHT IN THIS MONOCHROMATIC BATHROOM A PAIR OF FEATHERED TASSELS ENLIVENS A SHEER ROMAN BLIND, WHILE A TOWEL (FROM DAY BIRGER ET MIKKELSEN) ADDS A LOVELY TOUCH OF PATTERN AND SOFTNESS.

For a bathroom to be a place that satisfies those tricky dual requirements of an efficient space for cleansing and a sanctuary in which to relax, fabrics make all the difference. Not just in a practical sense, though obviously there are indispensable items such as screening at the windows and soft towels, but in an aesthetic sense, too. This room, by necessity, is furnished with ceramics and other cold, hard, shiny materials, and fabrics provide a balancing softness and warmth, without which the room would look awkward and feel uncomfortable.

If you want your bathroom fabrics to be and remain both useful and beautiful, there are certain types to avoid – in the main, anything very heavy or with a pile (other than towelling, of course) since it will hold moisture and, in a bathroom that gets very steamed up, possibly become mouldy and rotten. There are plenty of suitable fabrics, however, including lightweight cottons, linens and blends, all of which will dry quickly, and (depending how and where you wish to use them) synthetics, water-repellent or plasticized fabrics, plus fabrics used in other very watery areas, such as gabardine, oilcloth or even sailcloth (second-hand sails aren't particularly expensive and have plenty of areas you can cut out and use, as well as bold colours and lovely graphic numbers and letters).

Fabrics do not usually play a lavish part in a bathroom – perhaps more of a cameo – but they are, nevertheless, more evident than you might at first think.

WINDOW TREATMENTS

Even in a room that is not overlooked, you may wish to put up some form of window screening to keep the warmth in at night or simply to add some colour, pattern and a sense of comfort.

A no-nonsense, functional approach would be to use a roller blind, perhaps utilizing an interesting texture, a shaped cut-out on the bottom edge or at least an attractive blind-pull. Roman blinds, with their layers of elegant folds, tend to look a little more decorative, or you could go out on a limb and try some ruched blinds. In general, these went out of fashion in the 1980s, but, made from a sophisticated, plain fabric, they could look fabulous in an otherwise severe bathroom.

Full curtains are more tricky, but in a large or well-ventilated bathroom you should be able to get away with them. In small rooms, keep them simple. A pair of sheer café curtains (half-length curtains) on a rod or stretchy cord will shield you from prying eyes; for full-length curtains, you could use sheer or opaque fabric, without too much of a gather at the top – it is best to avoid the bunched-up, over-full look.

You may also decide to use curtains as an informal way to screen from view the contents of open-fronted cabinets or the underneath of a basin. Pastel gingham, vintage linen or intricate lace – there are all sorts of possibilities to suit the style of your room.

Curtains can also be used to surround an over-bath shower. In addition to the usual plastic curtain that keeps the shower water inside the bath, you can attach a length of hemmed fabric to the same pole or track and arrange it so that it hangs outside the bath. It is purely decorative, but does a good job at disguising a flappy, often mouldy bit of plastic, and coordinating with the rest of the room. In theory, these types of curtains should rarely get wet, but they

will suffer from occasional splashes, humidity and condensation, so it would be wise to use a quick-drying fabric such as light cotton or linen, and expect to replace them every few years.

ACCESSORIES

From face cloths and hand mitts to bath sheets and everything in between, towels are available in a bewildering array of choices. The most popular is cotton terry towelling, the best being made from heavyweight Egyptian cotton. For a refreshing rub-down, there is linen towelling, also known as friction or massage towelling, which is ultra-absorbent – as are the other alternatives of bamboo and hemp, each of which is said to be softer and more durable than cotton. Choose towels carefully, not just for fibre but also colour, texture and, if you wish, pattern, as they are usually a highly visible element of a bathroom and can make a substantial difference to its overall appearance. The 'eco' choices of organic cotton, linen, hemp and bamboo are usually available in undyed shades of grey, beige, cream and brown, which look gorgeous in a simple, understated or sophisticated space. Dyed cottons, on the other hand, come in every colour and can be perfectly coordinated to complement your scheme. Don't forget that you can opt for patterns and interesting details such as coloured borders or embroidery, or textures such as rib and waffle.

Finally, don't forget bathroom storage and seating. Storage might take the form of covered boxes, lined baskets or, especially in a family bathroom, drawstring bags hung from hooks or a peg rail. You could colour-code or embroider monograms if you wished to personalize them. Seating, depending

ABOVE Curtains can be used to screen a storage area below a washbasin. The smooth panel shown here, with its vintage buttons, has a pretty-but-practical air.

OPPOSITE Making a fabric shower curtain (lined with a plastic one for practicality) can introduce colour, pattern and personality into a bathroom. This ruffled example, made from Romo ticking, combines witty flair with a traditional style that suits its surroundings.

Introducing a few rough, nubbly or fluffy textures into a bathroom makes an interesting contrast with the smooth, shiny surfaces of ceramic, mirror and glass. Here, a seagrass massage mitt and fringed hand towel are ideal.

on space, could be a chaise longue, an armchair or a simple padded stool – a welcome place to relax or somewhere handy to sling your clothes. These seats aren't likely to suffer from much wear and tear, so fabrics needn't be especially tough and durable but, on the other hand, avoid anything delicate or expensive, in case of spills or splashes. You can't use plastic-coated fabrics (too slippery), but some synthetics or a tightly woven natural fabric will be inherently water-repellent. If making a slipcover, ideal for softening and disguising cheap timber or plastic chairs in a bathroom, you might use the same fabric as your window dressing, or even try towelling – perfect for absorbing moisture and can be hung on the line to dry out quickly and easily.

RIGHT A LAVISHLY DRAPED CURTAIN AND A DAYBED PILED WITH CUSHIONS GIVE THIS DRESSING ROOM A RESTFUL FEEL. THE FABRIC USED TO MAKE THE CUSHIONS IS BY FLORENCE BROADHURST, FROM TAPET-CAFÉ.

OPPOSITE, BELOW RIGHT A LITTLE EXTRA STORAGE IS ALWAYS WELCOME, AND THIS DRAWSTRING BAG, MADE FROM SEAGRASS AND RAFFIA, FROM ATELIER ABIGAIL AHERN, IS A USEFUL HOLDER FOR CLEAN TOWELS.

PRACTICALITIES: STORING TOWELS

It is easy to underestimate just how much space you will need to store towels, both towels in current use and fresh ones in waiting. Damp towels should always be aired and dried after use, and a heated towel rail or contemporary bathroom radiator is ideal for the purpose – just make sure that it is sizeable enough for all the family's towels, large and small. Failing that, a simple rail or row of hooks or towel rings above a radiator would be a cheap solution, as would be a traditional wood or bamboo rack that can be moved around as necessary.

Freshly laundered towels can be kept in an old-fashioned airing cupboard, if you are fortunate enough to have one, or else stacked or rolled on open shelves, in wire or wicker baskets or on a wall-mounted rack.

STYLE TIPS

Use fabrics to bring softness and comfort to a room that could otherwise be rather cold and stark. Choices that are both functional and beautiful include lightweight cottons and linens, towelling and sailcloth.

COLOURS in your bathroom might be subtle and muted - black, white and all the neutrals look lovely – but, if you wish, introduce a dash of brightness with floral or polka-dot patterned towels, a gingham blind or a ribbon-trimmed shower curtain.

WINDOWS are best kept relatively simple. However, if you want to make an exception, consider an eccentric ruched blind – lovely in antique linen and a great contrast to a sleek ceramic bathroom suite.

HIDE clutter with a simple screen. Make your own in the form of a gathered curtain or a flat panel hung across the front of an open cupboard or beneath a washbasin.

COVERED BOXES, lined baskets and drawstring bags all make cheap, good-looking and practical storage.

WORKROOMS & HOME OFFICES

If you have an office at home, make it as full of character as you wish. Who says swivel chairs have to be black or grey? Why can't an office curtain be as attractive as one in a living room? And why not have a few pretty accessories? If you can create an efficient space that also lifts your spirits, you will work more happily and, therefore, more effectively.

'The great thing about working from home is that you can
fashion your surroundings to suit your way of working,
designing the room around your personal preferences rather
than having to conform to a one-size-fits-all office plan.'

OPPOSITE, LEFT A GOOD LIGHT IS IMPORTANT TO WORK BY, AND ONE WITH AN ADJUSTABLE HINGED ARM IS IDEAL. THIS LINEN LAMPSHADE IS BY JOB INTERIEUR.

OPPOSITE, CENTRE SIMPLE DETAILS CAN MAKE ALL THE DIFFERENCE IN A WORK AREA — SUCH AS A PRETTY PADDED SEAT CUSHION, TIED ONTO THE CHAIR SO IT DOESN'T SLIP AROUND.

OPPOSITE, RIGHT DESIGNER PIET BOON'S HOME OFFICE IS INNATELY STYLISH, WITH ELEGANT CURTAINS CONSISTING OF A LAYER EACH OF LINEN AND SILK.

A home office may not seem the obvious place for decorative fabrics — and frilly, flouncy styles would definitely look out of place in a streamlined home-business venue — but you may be surprised by what scope there is for improving your work environment.

If you have chosen to work from home, it is, presumably, partly because you want to avoid the dull monotony of corporate spaces. Corporate office fabrics are chosen because they are tough and durable; you should choose your home office fabrics because you love them and they make you feel good. If you are using the room on a daily basis, however, don't buy anything too delicate — think of the types of fabric you would choose for living-room window treatments or sofas and you will be on the right track. For people who can't concentrate unless everything around them is calm and serene, neutral, plain fabrics might be best; otherwise, joyful colours and lively patterns may fit the bill (avoiding clashes and anything too garish, of course), as they will be used in relatively small doses so shouldn't become overwhelming.

WINDOW TREATMENTS & ROOM DIVIDERS

Depending on where you work and what you do, you may wish to look out through a bare window over an attractive view — or you may require a curtain or blind to maintain your privacy, in which case sheer curtains, half-length or full, should serve the purpose adequately during the day, with an additional blind or curtain made of thicker, opaque fabric for use after dark.

Hang roman blinds high enough above the window so that they don't obscure the top of it when pulled up. If you have chosen curtains rather than blinds, make sure the pole or track extends far enough each side of the window to be able to pull the fabric right back and allow maximum light inside. Also, don't let curtains dangle over your desk or your work; elaborate floor-length drapes are no good if they swish across your file boxes every time you pull them. Thick, thermally lined window dressings are ideal in a work room that tends to get chilly; close them before dusk for maximum effect.

In any office, home or otherwise, there will be some things that you're happy to show off, and quite a lot that

ABOVE IMPRESSIVE CURTAINS NEED NOT COST THE EARTH. THESE HAVE BEEN MADE FROM WHITE COTTON, BUT THEIR LARGE EYELETS THREADED OVER A METAL POLE MAKE THEM LOOK EXTREMELY CHIC.

OPPOSITE ROMAN BLINDS CAN BE ADJUSTED TO INCREASE PRIVACY OR REDUCE GLARE, ARE EASY TO MAKE AND DON'T USE A GREAT DEAL OF FABRIC – WHICH MEANS THEY LOOK EFFECTIVE WITHOUT BEING EXCESSIVELY EXPENSIVE.

you'd rather hide away. The great thing about working from home is that you can fashion your surroundings to suit your way of working, designing the room around your personal preferences rather than to conform to a one-size-fits-all office plan. So, while there's no substitute for well-made wooden or metal cupboards and shelves for storing files, books and boxes, you can use fabric, too, to disguise your storage. When your office is in a spare room, your storage may well consist of built-in shelves either side of a fireplace, or perhaps some cheap and cheerful flatpack shelves without doors. And when open shelves look too utilitarian – which especially applies if you're combining a work room with a living area and need to hide the evidence of your day job in the evenings – simply make a gathered or flat-panel curtain to hang over them, either from top to bottom or beneath a lower-down shelf. Either hooks or a small track would work well; on tall cupboards, the alternative might be a roller or roman blind. Use a fabric that's the same colour as the woodwork or walls if you want it to blend in; alternatively, choose a pattern or colour that has more personality and makes you feel happy and inspired.

FURNITURE

Your office chair is the linchpin of all your home working activities, whether you are sitting at a computer, a sewing machine or a soldering iron. As such, it must be chosen with care, particularly if you will be spending many hours

Workroom storage is essential. A simple set of shelves is often the most straightforward, affordable solution, and if you don't want to look at what's kept on them, a curtain makes the ideal screen. You could make a curtain that extends from ceiling to floor, or one that simply covers part of the shelving, and suspend it from a slender pole, track, rod or wire. Choose a colour and pattern that either blend into the background or coordinate with your overall scheme.

each day sitting in it. Manufacturers of the standard swivel chair have just, and only just, come around to the idea that an interesting fabric cover actually appeals to some people, and if you are fortunate you may be able to find a chair that coordinates well with the rest of your room. If not, it's up to you to make a slipcover, in a fabric that is reasonably hard-wearing, neither too rough nor too slippery, and without a deep pile or a loopy weave. If you're in an extravagant mood (and why not?), consider moleskin, corduroy, low-pile velvet and felt;

otherwise, medium- to heavyweight cottons and cotton mixes, linen mixes and wools would be perfect. A daring option would be to choose a bold pattern, perhaps a floral, something graphically abstract or a retro design, but for those who want a quieter life, soft pastels or neutrals would be ideal.

Seat cushions and pads may be either an indulgence or a necessity, but they are certainly a good way to show off some attractive fabrics and they help pull a room scheme together – even in a practical space such as this.

On an attractive wooden or metal chair, a cushion could be the crowning glory; make sure it fits both the width and depth of the seat so it doesn't slip around and annoy you. Ties are often advisable. Since you are unlikely to need an enormous amount of fabric, you can make cushion covers from remnants or small lengths of very expensive material, and perhaps finish them with quirky touches such as ruffles, ric rac, bows or buttons.

ACCESSORIES

Fabrics can be used in ingenious ways for home office storage – and they really come into their own if your working area is a craft-oriented space in which you sew, knit or crochet, make jewellery, paint or carry out any other activity which requires storing an abundance of small items from cotton reels or embroidery needles to beads or brushes. Boxes and files, which seem to proliferate and are not necessarily particularly attractive in themselves, can be covered with fabric to give them a more homely appearance, or simply to disguise disparate styles and put together a coordinated look. Baskets, meanwhile, can be lined with fabric to provide a smooth inside surface for storage. Drawstring bags, hung from hooks or a peg rail, may be used to contain a variety of items, while even the humble jam jar, which may be used to store buttons, paper clips or whatever, can be jazzed up with miniature scraps of fabric covering the lids. Lastly, for an informal memo board, you could stretch a length of fabric over inexpensive cork board, and criss-cross it with pretty ribbons.

PRACTICALITIES: USING COLOUR AND PATTERN IN A HOME OFFICE

If you work from home, you can decorate your office to suit yourself, but it is worth considering before you start how your environment will affect your work. Zingy shades and bold designs may perk you up at first, but will they get on your nerves after a few weeks? On the other hand, if you play it safe and go beige, will it all feel rather dull?

By keeping walls and floors neutral, you can experiment by adding fabrics, in the form of cushions or chair covers, door stops, blinds, lampshades, file covers and so on, and gradually get a feel for what suits you best. Touches of colour and pattern can be repeated in other areas, such as painted shelves, a rug, a painting or a collection of vases, until the result is a unified and attractive whole that is really conducive to effective and enjoyable work.

ABOVE Even a straightforward filing tray can be given a dash of lively chic by covering it with a zingy fabric.

LEFT Jam jars with fabric-covered lids make ideal storage for small items such as buttons, drawing pins or cotton reels.

FAR LEFT Remnants can be used to cover plain boxes as storage for pens, pencils and other stationery.

OPPOSITE In this young person's work space, a simple wooden desk and chairs are matched with unfussy fabric storage: a linen-covered noticeboard, drawstring bags and a linen-lined hanging basket.

WORKROOMS & HOME OFFICES **135**

STYLE TIPS

Make your home work area
both luxurious and interesting
by using fabrics that charm and
inspire. Day-to-day function
and comfort are paramount,
of course, but this is also a
space that you can make
entirely your own, expressing
your individuality with colour,
pattern and intriguing touches.

PATTERN can be used in small doses to enliven and enrich a home
office – unless, of course, you're allergic to it, in which case use a
glorious range of textures instead.

FABRIC SCREENS are as easy to make as any simple gathered
curtain and can either blend into the background or stand out as
a feature. They'll hide your clutter but leave it easily accessible.

OFFICE CHAIRS should never be dull and boring. Get the
ergonomics right, then add a gorgeous cover to liven things up.

SMALL ACCESSORIES make a big difference. Cover boxes, files,
noticeboards, even jam-jar lids with coordinating fabrics for a soft
and welcoming look.

OUTDOOR SPACES

Warm sunshine and blue skies are not the only
ingredients for a perfect summer's day spent out
of doors. A comfortable spot in which to lounge
– reading, listening to music, chatting or dozing –
and a pleasant place in which to sit and eat with
family or friends are vital. And a spot of shade –
be it from a chic parasol, a grand awning or an
informal length of sailcloth – is always welcome.

'A chic look is easy to achieve using neutral colours such as off-white, stone, taupe or, for the slightly more daring, charcoal. Shades of blue are always attractive, but green may be difficult to get right, since it can clash with the greens in your foliage.'

Whether your outdoor space is a small balcony, an urban patio or a vast country garden, or an indoor–outdoor space such as a veranda, summerhouse or porch, fabrics can complement chairs, tables, sun loungers and other exterior furnishings and help to create a useful, as well as good-looking, area for relaxation.

Outdoor fabrics can be divided into two types: the ones that are brought indoors when not in use and those that are left outside most, or perhaps all, of the time. The former may be made from almost any sturdy conventional fabric, such as cotton, heavy linen, canvas and denim. Delicates are best avoided since you never know when someone might throw a cushion on the floor or jump on a lounger with muddy feet. Provided you allow these fabrics to air thoroughly if they become damp, and store them somewhere dry (garden sheds aren't always the best places for keeping fabric), they should be fine.

If you plan to leave seat covers, cushions, deckchairs, hammocks, awnings and so on outside, on the other hand, you will have to choose fabrics that can cope with the twin enemies of sunshine and water. Bright light is liable to make most conventional fabrics fade, and will accelerate deterioration; while damp, if not attended to quickly enough, usually causes mildew and rot. None of these developments is reversible. There are specialist fabrics on the market which have been treated to make them resistant to ultraviolet light, stains, water and mildew, or you can buy silicone sprays, from camping, outdoor or hardware stores, which are easy to apply yourself. Do check first on a small area, though, to see how it affects the surface finish, colour, feel and drape of the fabric, and bear in mind that you may need to reapply it at regular intervals. Alternatively, choose fabrics that are inherently waterproof or water-repellent, such as some acrylics, polyesters and nylons, or vinyl-laminated fabrics (usually called oilcloth), which will wipe clean and dry. More unusual choices include rubber, neoprene (wetsuit material) and sailcloth.

As for colour and pattern, most people tend to be bolder in their outdoor choices than they would be when decorating the inside of their homes. This is a chance to express yourself in an uninhibited way, and it's true that

THIS PICTURE BOTH INDOORS AND OUT, IT'S
POSSIBLE TO USE FABRICS TO CREATE A MIXTURE
OF COLOURS, PATTERNS AND TEXTURES THAT IS
VISUALLY AND SENSUALLY APPEALING. HERE,
A QUILTED THROW, INDIAN FABRIC BOLSTER,
SEQUINNED CUSHIONS AND LINEN TICKING
ARE COMBINED IN A RELAXED AND STYLISH
OUTDOOR SEATING AREA TO GREAT EFFECT.

dramatic fabrics can look fabulous in a garden setting – but there is no excuse for cheap and cheerful, garish colours or hideous, clashing patterns. A chic look is easy to achieve using neutral colours such as off-white, stone, taupe or, for the slightly more daring, charcoal. Shades of blue are always attractive, but green may be difficult to get right, since it can clash badly with all the greens in your foliage. The overall style of your garden will set the tone for colour, and also pattern, which may take the form of deckchair stripes, pretty gingham, chintzy florals or perhaps something graphic, organic or ethnic. A well-chosen mixture of patterns and colours – a couple of plains, some tiny checks and a floral or two, for example – will look gorgeous in the right setting, or you could be more restrained and stick to plains/solids and maybe just a simple stripe.

FURNITURE

It is rare to use upholstered furniture in an outdoor setting – though it may be possible in a dry summerhouse or well-covered veranda. Instead, using slipcovers, seat pads and cushions is the ideal way to bring softness and comfort to wood, metal or plastic chairs and benches, with the added advantage that they are easy to take off and wash, dry and store. Or there's the simplest option of all: a length of cloth thrown over a seat for a totally relaxed and easy look. Slipcovers can be made in the same way as those for indoor seating, and may be tailored so that they pull on and fit quite well, or be less structured and fastened with ties, buttons or poppers. Box-shaped pads are great tied onto chair seats, and larger, quilted pads can be used on top of sun loungers or as

ABOVE This very stylish indoor–outdoor space belongs to Dutch designer Piet Boon. The two areas are separated by the contrasting colours of the woodwork, but the grey upholstery unifies them and provides a crisp, tailored look.

ABOVE RIGHT Even in midsummer, evenings can become chilly, so when dining outside a soft throw is ideal for pulling around you when temperatures drop.

mattresses on the ground. Meanwhile, if you have long benches, you can pile cushions and bolsters up so they look appealing and can be sunk into whenever the need arises. And don't forget table linens. Tablecloths, runners, place mats and napkins should complement cushions or chair covers and will transform an outdoor dining area into a truly special place.

AWNINGS & EXTRAS

By adding an awning to an exterior wall or erecting a freestanding canopy in the garden, you can create a new 'room' for entertaining or relaxing or as a children's play area. There are plenty of companies that will sell you a grand, retractable awning with permanent fixings, the most impressive of which are operated by remote control and even fitted with sun and wind sensors. If

you are so inclined, however, it would not be particularly difficult to rig up something of your own – perhaps not quite so long-lasting, but potentially more individual and charming. Using an outdoor fabric of the type mentioned above (sailcloth is particularly attractive, with its bold colours and graphic lettering and numbers), you can either make eyelets or sew on ties which you can attach to hooks on convenient walls or nearby trees; just unhook or untie it if you're not likely to use it for a while. To make a simple tent for the youngsters to play in, throw a large piece of fabric over a low-hanging branch, or tie it in the centre and suspend as a tepee. Fabric finishing touches include hammocks, deckchairs and colourful bunting, in glorious colours and appealing patterns, for a beautiful, useable space that children and adults alike will enjoy all summer long.

ABOVE FABRICS WILL FADE IF YOU LEAVE THEM IN THE SUN, BUT IN MANY CASES THIS DOESN'T DO THEM ANY HARM. INDEED, IT SOMETIMES MAKES THEM EVEN PRETTIER – AS WITH THIS CATH KIDSTON PRINT, WHOSE VINTAGE STYLE IS IDEAL FOR A WORN, RUSTIC LOOK.

ABOVE LEFT RELAXATION AND ELEGANCE ARE COMBINED IN THIS ALFRESCO DINING SCENE. A GENEROUS CANVAS PARASOL PROTECTS DINERS FROM THE SUN AND THE CHIC PINSTRIPE OF THE COTTON TABLECLOTH IS REFLECTED IN THE SEAT CUSHIONS. A TAN CASHMERE THROW ADDS AN ELEMENT OF SOFTNESS.

RIGHT Pale, square seat covers, in a heavy-duty canvas fabric suitable for permanent outdoor use, make this seating area by Marijke van Nunen crisp and clean. For a bit of fun and frivolity, though, she has added a selection of cushions covered in vibrantly coloured and patterned fabrics. These can easily be stored safely away in inclement weather.

STYLE TIPS

Vivid colours and patterns tend to be the norm for outdoor schemes. But sophisticated neutrals and soft pastels can also look gorgeous in the right setting, providing comfortable seating, enjoyable dining and some welcome shade.

CHOOSE the right fabric for the right place. As long as you can bring the item indoors when not in use, the fabric simply needs to be reasonably hard-wearing; if it's going to be left out a great deal, however, you'll need to consider water-resistant or specially treated fabrics.

SEAT COVERS can set a strong style. Neatly tailored versions in neutral colours are boldly minimal, while looser ones in soft colours, or even patterns, are more relaxed. Brighter colours introduce a cheerful note, but beware of clashes with your foliage and flowers.

USE THROWS and blankets as informal covers for seats and benches; they can also keep you warm on a chilly summer's evening.

MAKE AWNINGS, canopies and tents yourself from sturdy fabric, with eyelets or ties to attach them to walls or tree branches.

Most of the fabric companies listed here sell or supply their products in both the UK and the USA. Call them or visit their websites for more information.

Anthropologie
www.anthropologie.com
Ethic and vintage-inspired home accessories, including bedspreads, rugs, cushions and throws.

Atelier Abigail Ahern
12–14 Essex Road
London N1 8LN
+ 44 (0)7354 8181
www.atelierabigailahern.com
Quirky mixture of objects for contemporary interiors.

Barneys New York
www.barneys.com
High-quality home furnishings.

Bedside Manor
www.bedsidemanor.com
Fine blankets, bedspreads, linens and other bedroom accessories.

Bennison Fabrics
www.bennisonfabric.com
Timeless hand-printed fabrics based on 18th and 19th-century English and French textiles. All fabrics can also be printed as wallpaper.

Blithfield
www.blithfield.co.uk
Colourful printed and woven furnishing fabrics and wallpapers, including the Peggy Angus collection of hand-blocked linen.

Borderline Fabrics
www.borderlinefabrics.com
Inspired textile collections from archival to retro designs.

Brissi
196 Westbourne Grove
London W11 2RH
+ 44 (0)20 7727 2159
www.brissi.co.uk
Chic furniture and tableware.

Cabbages & Roses
6 West Street
Midhurst
West Sussex GU29 9NQ
www.cabbagesandroses.com
Pretty floral fabrics.

Calico Corners
www.calicocorners.com
Over 100 retail outlets across the USA.

Cath Kidston
www.cathkidston.co.uk
Vintage-style prints.

The Cloth House
47 Berwick Street
London W1F 8SJ
+ 44 (0)20 7437 5155
www.clothhouse.com
A vast range of natural fabrics and vintage trimmings.

The Cloth Shop
290 Portobello Road
London W10 5TE
+ 44 (0)20 8968 6001
Specializes in antique fabrics, French and Swedish linens, Indian fabrics, Welsh blankets, Italian fabrics and English wool.

Colefax and Fowler
110 Fulham Road
London SW3 6HU, UK
+ 44 (0)20 7244 7427
www.colefax.com
Classic, timeless fabrics from the legendary British brand.

The Conran Shop
www.conran.com
Inspired blend of modern, classic, vintage and ethnic interiors. A carefully curated edit of textiles, including washed linen bedding and bold cushions and throws.

Cowtan & Tout
www.cowtan.com
Home furnishing fabrics from Colefax and Fowler, Cowtan & Tout, Jane Churchill, Larsen and Manuel Canovas.

Crate & Barrel
www.crateandbarrel.com
Pillows, throws and bedlinens with a contemporary appeal.

Décors Barbares by Nathalie Farman-Farma
www.decorsbarbares.com
Textile designs inspired by traditional Persian, central Asian and Russian costumes.

Designers Guild
267 & 277 Kings Road
London SW3 5EN, UK
+ 44 (0)20 7351 5775
www.designersguild.com
Bold and vibrant furnishing fabrics by Tricia Guild.

Elanbach
www.elanbach.com
Digitally printed fabrics, from florals to stripes.

Fanny Shorter
www.fannyshorter.com
Vibrant and colourful printed linens and cottons.

Fermoie
53–55 Pimlico Road
London SW1W 8NE
+ 44 (0)1672 513723
www.fermoie.com
*Pure cotton and linen
fabrics suitable for upholstery,
draper, fabric walling and
other interior uses. Also
coordinating cushions
and lampshades.*

George Smith
www.georgesmith.com
*High-quality upholstered
sofas, chairs and stools.*

Graham & Green
www.grahamandgreen.co.uk
Home accessories.

Habitat
www.habitat.net
*Good-value ready-made
blinds, cushions and soft
furnishings*

Heal's
+ 44 (0)20 7636 1666
www.heals.co.uk
*Contemporary fabrics and
soft furnishings.*

Ian Mankin
269–271 Wandsworth Bridge
Road
London SW6 2TX
+ 44 (0)20 7722 0997
www.ianmankin.com
Tickings and utility fabrics.

John Lewis
www.johnlewis.com
*Department store with more
than 25 branches nationwide
and an excellent fabric range.*

Katharine Pole
www.katharinepole.com
+ 44 (0)7757 616692
*French antiques, decorative
objects and rare textiles.*

Laura Ashley
www.lauraashley.com
*Cotton fabrics with English
garden look. Coordinated
pillows, bedding and trims.*

Lewis & Wood
www.lewisandwood.co.uk
*Beautiful and unusual fabrics
and wallpapers.*

Luma
98 Church Road
London SW13 0DQ
+ 44 (0)20 8748 2264
www.lumadirect.com
*Luxury organic bed linen
and soft furnishings.*

Lunn Antiques
www.lunnantiques.com
*Great selection of antique
lace and textiles.*

MacCulloch & Wallis
25–26 Poland Street
London W1F 8QN
www.macculloch-wallis.co.uk
*Ribbons, trimmings and
fashion accessories plus
fabrics and sewing equipment.*

Malabar
www.malabar.co.uk
*Indian-inspired furnishing
fabrics.*

Marijke van Nunen
www.mvninteriors.com
Beautiful furnishings.

Molly Mahon
www.mollymahon.com
*Colourful, cheerful block-
printed fabric plus cushions,
bedding, table linen and
lampshades.*

Osborne & Little
304 Kings Road
London SW3 5UH, UK
www.osborneandlittle.com
*Stylish fabrics, wallpapers
and trimmings.*

Pottery Barn
www.potterybarn.com
*Modern furnishings and
home accents.*

Romo Fabrics
www.romofabrics.com
*Classic and contemporary
fabrics, wallpapers and
trimmings with an extensive
choice of plains and stripes.*

Samarkand Design
www.samarkanddesign.com
*Lampshades made from
antique silk sarees or
hand-blocked cotton voile.*

Scalamandré
www.scalamandre.com
*Legendary American
decorative textile brand
producing their own fabrics
as well as representing many
renowned international brands.*

Southsea Deckchairs
www.deckchairs.co.uk
*Wide range of different styles
of deckchair.*

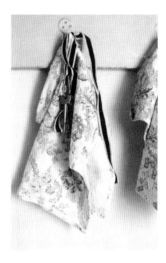

Streett Marburg
297 Lillie Road
London SW6 7LL
+ 44 (0)20 7381 4344
Streettmarburg.co.uk
*Antique textiles, cushions
and bolsters.*

Toast
www.toa.st
*Relaxed and stylish
homewares and soft
furnishings, including
washed linen bedding.*

Volga Linen
www.volgalinen.co.uk
*Luxury linen products for
the home and pure linen
by the metre.*

Zoffany
www.zoffany.com
*Sophisticated range of
fabrics and trimmings.*

PICTURE CREDITS

All photography by Lisa Cohen unless otherwise stated.
key: a=above, b=below, r=right, l=left, c=centre, ph=photographer.

Endpapers Cloth House, 47 Berwick Street, London W1F 8SJ www.clothhouse.com;

1 Owner of Tapet Café, Textile Designer Helene Blanche and husband and Jannik Martensen-Larsen; **2** The home of Nina Hartmann www.vintagebynina.com; **3** The home of designer Marijke van Nunen; **4 a** The home of Nina Hartmann www.vintagebynina.com; **4 c** Cloth House, 47 Berwick Street, London W1F 8SJ. www.clothhouse.com; **4 b** Designer Rose Uniacke's home in London; **5 a** Kate Forman's home; **5 c** The home of Lars Wiberg of Pour Quoi in Copenhagen; **5 b** The home of Nina Hartmann www.vintagebynina.com; **6 r** Chair designed by Jane Cumberbatch, www.purestyleonline.com; **9** The home of Lars Wiberg of Pour Quoi in Copenhagen; **10–11** An apartment in Amsterdam designed by Marijke van Nunen; **12 a & bc** Cloth House, 47 Berwick Street, London W1F 8SJ. www.clothhouse.com; **12 bl** The home of Chris van Eldik and Wendy Jansen of J.O.B. Interieurs; **12 br** The home of designer Marijke van Nunen; **13** Cloth House, 47 Berwick Street, London W1F 8SJ. www.clothhouse.com; **14 l** The home of Lars Wiberg of Pour Quoi in Copenhagen; **14 r** Ph Claire Richardson/ 'Madison', 'Luna' & ''Knot Garden' cushions and throws by Melin Tregwynt; **15 l** An apartment in Amsterdam designed by Marijke van Nunen; **15 r** The home in London of Abigail Ahern, www.atelierabigailahern.com; **16 ar** Cloth House, 47 Berwick Street, London W1F 8SJ. www.clothhouse.com; **16 a c** Ph Paul Massey/ Naja Lauf; **16 bl** Chairs designed by Jane Cumberbatch, www.purestyleonline.com; **16 br** Tablecloth designed by Jane Cumberbatch, www.purestyleonline.com; **18 l** The home of designer Marijke van Nunen; **18 c & br** Kate Forman's home; **18 bc** The home of Lars Wiberg of Pour Quoi in Copenhagen; **20 al** The home of Chris van Eldik and Wendy Jansen of J.O.B. Interieurs; **20 ac** Cloth House, 47 Berwick Street, London W1F 8SJ. www.clothhouse.com; **20 ar** The home of Lars Wiberg of Pour Quoi in Copenhagen; **20 bl & br** Cloth House, 47 Berwick Street, London W1F 8SJ. www.clothhouse.com; **20 bc** Clara Baillie's house on the Isle of Wight; **21** The home of Chris van Eldik and Wendy Jansen of J.O.B. Interieurs; **22** Cloth House, 47 Berwick Street, London W1F 8SJ. www.clothhouse.com; **23** The home of designer Marijke van Nunen; **24** Cloth House, 47 Berwick Street, London W1F 8SJ. www.clothhouse.com; **25** The home of Nina Hartmann www.vintagebynina.com; **26 l** Designer Rose Uniacke's home in London; **26 c** Cloth House, 47 Berwick Street, London W1F 8SJ. www.clothhouse.com; **26 r** The home of designer Marijke van Nunen; **27** Anna McDougall's London home; **28–29** The designers Piet & Karin Boon's home near Amsterdam, www.pietboon.nl; **30**
The designer Clare Teed's home in Hampton, www.sashawaddell.com; **32 l & c** Kate Forman's home; **36** The designer Clare Teed's home in Hampton, www.sashawaddell.com; **38 a** Owner of Tapet Café, Textile Designer Helene Blanche and husband and Jannik Martensen-Larsen; **38 b** Designer Rose Uniacke's home in London; **39** Ph Polly Wreford/ www.susanchalom.com **40–41** An apartment in Amsterdam designed by Marijke van Nunen; **42 l** The home of Chris van Eldik and Wendy Jansen of J.O.B. Interieurs; **42 c** Designer Rose Uniacke's home in London; **42 r** The designer Clare Teed's home in Hampton, www.sashawaddell.com; **43** Anna Mcdougall's London home; **44 l** The home of Chris van Eldik and Wendy Jansen of J.O.B. Interieurs; **44 r** Designer Rose Uniacke's home in London; **45 l** The home in London of Abigail Ahern, www.atelierabigailahern.com; **45 r** Designer Rose Uniacke's home in London; **46 a l** The home of Nina Hartmann www.vintagebynina.com; **46 a c** Owner of Tapet Café, Textile Designer Helene Blanche and husband and Jannik Martensen-Larsen; **46 a r & b c** Anna Mcdougall's London home; **46 br** The home of Nina Hartmann www.vintagebynina.com; **47** Anna Mcdougall's London home; **48 l** The home of Lars Wiberg of Pour Quoi in Copenhagen; **48 r** Clara Baillie's house on the Isle of Wight; **49 a** Designer Rose Uniacke's home in London; **49 b** The designers Piet & Karin Boon's home near Amsterdam, www.pietboon.nl; **50 l** An apartment in Amsterdam designed by Marijke van Nunen; **50 c** The home of Nina Hartmann www.vintagebynina.com; **50 r** Owner of Tapet Café, Textile Designer Helene Blanche and husband and Jannik Martensen-Larsen; **51** The designer Clare Teed's home in Hampton, www.sashawaddell.com; **52** The home of Nina Hartmann www.vintagebynina.com; **54 l** An apartment in Amsterdam designed by Marijke van Nunen; **54 c** The home of designer Marijke van Nunen; **54 r** The home of Lars Wiberg of Pour Quoi in Copenhagen; **58** Clara Baillie's house on the Isle of Wight; **60** The home of Lars Wiberg of Pour Quoi in Copenhagen; **61 c** The home of designer Marijke van Nunen; **62 l** The designer Clare Teed's home in Hampton, www.sashawaddell.com; **62 r** The home of Lars Wiberg of Pour Quoi in Copenhagen; **63 l** T Owner of Tapet Café, Textile Designer Helene Blanche and husband and Jannik Martensen-Larsen; **63 r** The designers Piet & Karin Boon's home near Amsterdam, www.pietboon.nl; **64** The designer Clare Teed's home in Hampton, www.sashawaddell.com; **66–67** The home of Nina Hartmann www.vintagebynina.com; **68–69** Ph Claire Richardson/ black & white chinaware by Missoni, cushions and tablecloth by Marimekko; **70 l** Ph Paul Massey/ Jan Constantine –

www.janconstantine.com; **70 r** The home of Chris van Eldik and Wendy Jansen of J.O.B. Interieurs; **71 l** Ph Paul Massey/ Hôtel Le Sénéchal, Ars en Ré, designed by Christophe Ducharme Architecte; **71 r** Ph Polly Wreford/ London home of Michael Bains and Catherine Woram; **72 & 73 r** Anna Mcdougall's London home; **74 l** The home of designer Marijke van Nunen; **74 c** The home of Lars Wiberg of Pour Quoi in Copenhagen; **74 r** Designer Rose Uniacke's home in London; **75** The home of Nina Hartmann www.vintagebynina.com; **77 b** Kate Forman's home; **78 c** Kate Forman's home; **78 r** The home of Nina Hartmann www.vintagebynina.com; **79** Designer Rose Uniacke's home in London; **80** Kate Forman's home; **82 l & r** Kate Forman's home; **84 l** The designer Clare Teed's home in Hampton, www.sashawaddell.com; **84 r** Owner of Tapet Café, Textile Designer Helene Blanche and husband and Jannik Martensen-Larsen; **85** Designer Rose Uniacke's home in London; **87** Ph Paul Massey/ The home in Denmark of Charlotte Lyngaard, designer of Ole Lyngaard; **88–89** The home of Lars Wiberg of Pour Quoi in Copenhagen; **90–91** The designer Clare Teed's home in Hampton, www.sashawaddell.com; **93** Anna Mcdougall's London home; **96 l & c** The designers Piet & Karin Boon's home near Amsterdam, www.pietboon.nl; **96 r** The home of Chris van Eldik and Wendy Jansen of J.O.B. Interieurs; **97** The home in London of Abigail Ahern, www.atelierabigailahern.com; **98** The designer Clare Teed's home in Hampton, www.sashawaddell.com; **99 l & c** An apartment in Amsterdam designed by Marijke van Nunen; **99 r** The designers Piet & Karin Boon's home near Amsterdam, www.pietboon.nl; **101** The home of Lars Wiberg of Pour Quoi in Copenhagen; **102** Ph Debi Treloar/ Sophie Eadie's family home in London; **103** Ph Debi Treloar/ Christine Tholstrup Hermansen and Helge Drencks house in Copenhagen; **104** The home of Nina Hartmann www.vintagebynina.com; **105** Owner of Tapet Café, Textile Designer Helene Blanche and husband and Jannik Martensen-Larsen; **106 r** The home of designer Marijke van Nunen; **107 l** The designers Piet & Karin Boon's home near Amsterdam, www.pietboon.nl; **107 r** Owner of Tapet Café, Textile Designer Helene Blanche and husband and Jannik Martensen-Larsen; **108** The home of Lars Wiberg of Pour Quoi in Copenhagen; **109 a** The home of designer Marijke van Nunen; **109 b** The home of Lars Wiberg of Pour Quoi in Copenhagen; **110 c** The designer Clare Teed's home in Hampton, www.sashawaddell.com; **110 r** Kate Forman's home; **111** The home of Nina Hartmann www.vintagebynina.com; **112** The designer Clare Teed's home in Hampton, www.sashawaddell.com; **114 l** The designers Piet & Karin Boon's home near Amsterdam, www.pietboon.nl; **114 c** The home of Chris van Eldik and Wendy Jansen of J.O.B. Interieurs;

114 r The home of Lars Wiberg of Pour Quoi in Copenhagen; **116** The home of Nina Hartmann www.vintagebynina.com; **117** Ph Polly Wreford/ Sahsa Waddell's home available from www.beachstudios.co.uk; **119** The designer Clare Teed's home in Hampton, www.sashawaddell.com; **120** The home in London of Abigail Ahern, www.atelierabigailahern.com; **121** Owner of Tapet Café, Textile Designer Helene Blanche and husband and Jannik Martensen-Larsen; **122 l** The home of Nina Hartmann www.vintagebynina.com; **122 r** The home of Chris van Eldik and Wendy Jansen of J.O.B. Interieurs; **123** Anna Mcdougall's London home; **124** The home of Nina Hartmann www.vintagebynina.com; **126 l** The home of Chris van Eldik and Wendy Jansen of J.O.B. Interieurs; **126 r** The designers Piet & Karin Boon's home near Amsterdam, www.pietboon.nl; **128** Owner of Tapet Café, Textile Designer Helene Blanche and husband and Jannik Martensen-Larsen; **130** Jane Cumberbatch, www.purestyleonline.com; **131** Clara Baillie's house on the Isle of Wight; **133** Kate Forman's home; **134–135 l** The home of Nina Hartmann www.vintagebynina.com; **135 c** Clara Baillie's house on the Isle of Wight; **136 l** Owner of Tapet Café, Textile Designer Helene Blanche and husband and Jannik Martensen-Larsen; **136 c & r** The home in London of Abigail Ahern, www.atelierabigailahern.com; **138** The designers Piet & Karin Boon's home near Amsterdam, www.pietboon.nl; **140 l & r** The home of designer Marijke van Nunen; **140 c** Ph Debi Treloar/ Dar Beida and Dar Emma, available to rent – www.castlesinthesand.com, interior designers Emma Wilson and Graham Carter; **142–143** The home of Lars Wiberg of Pour Quoi in Copenhagen; **144 l** The designers Piet & Karin Boon's home near Amsterdam, www.pietboon.nl; **144 r** The home of Lars Wiberg of Pour Quoi in Copenhagen; **145 l** Ph Paul Massey/ The home in Denmark of Charlotte Lyngaard, designer of Ole Lyngaard; **145 r** Clara Baillie's house on the Isle of Wight; **146–147** The home of designer Marijke van Nunen; **148 l** The home of designer Marijke van Nunen; Clara Baillie's house on the Isle of Wight; **148 r** The designers Piet & Karin Boon's home near Amsterdam, www.pietboon.nl; **149** Ph Debi Treloar/ Dar Beida and Dar Emma, available to rent – www.castlesinthesand.com, interior designers Emma Wilson and Graham Carter; **150** Clara Baillie's house on the Isle of Wight; **151** Kate Forman's home; **153** Designer Rose Uniacke's home in London; **154** The home in London of Abigail Ahern, www.atelierabigailahern.com; **157** Anna McDougall's London home; **160 a l** The home of Lars Wiberg of Pour Quoi in Copenhagen; **160 a c & b** Cloth House, 47 Berwick Street, London W1F 8SJ www.clothhouse.com; **160 a r** The home of Chris van Eldik and Wendy Jansen of J.O.B. Interieurs.

BUSINESS CREDITS

key: a=above, b=below, l=left, r=right, c=centre.

Atelier Abigail Ahem
137 Upper Street
Islington
London N1 1QP, UK
t: + 44 (0)20 7354 8181
e: contact@atelierbypost.com
www.atelierabigailahern.com
Pages 15 r, 45 l, 97, 120, 136
c & r, 154.

Beach Studios
t: + 44 (0)1797 344077
e: office@beachstudios.co.uk
www.beachstudios.co.uk
and
Sasha Waddell Interior Design
& Lectures
www.sashawaddelldesign.com
Page 117.

Cloth House
47 Berwick Street
London W1F 8SJ, UK
www.clothhouse.com
Endpapers, pages 4 c, 12 a &
be, 13, 16 ar, 20 ac, 20 bl & br,
22, 24, 26 c, 160 ac, 160 b.

Helene Blanche Martensen-
Larsen
Tapet Café
Brogårdsvej 23
DK-2820 Gentofte
Denmark
t: + 45 396 56630
e: info@tapet-cafe.dk
www.tapet-cafe.dk
Pages 1, 38 a, 46 ac, 50 r,
63 l, 84 r, 105, 109 r, 128,
138 l.

Hôtel Le Sénéchal
6 rue Gambetta
Ars en Ré
France
T: + 33 (0)5 46 29 40 42
www.hotel-le-senechal.com
designed by Christophe
Ducharme Architecte
15 rue Hégésippe Moreau
75018 Paris
France
t: +33 (0)1 45 22 07 75
71 l.

Jan Constantine
t: + 44 (0)1270 821194
www.janconstantine.com
Page 70.

Jane Cumberbatch
www.purestyleonline.com
Pages 6 r, 16 bl, 16 br, 130.

JOB Interieurs
Oeverstraat 21
3961 AA Wijk bij Duurstede
The Netherlands
t: + 31 343 578818
e: jobint@xs4all.nl
Pages 12 bl, 20 al, 21, 42 l,
44 l, 70 r, 96 r, 114 c, 122 r,
126 l, 160 ar.

Kate Forman Designs
Long Barn North
Sutton Manor Farm
Bishops Sutton
Alresford
Hampshire SO24 0AA, UK
t: + 44 (0)1962 732244
e: kate@kateforman.co.uk
www.kateforman.co.uk
Pages 5 a, 18 b, 32 l & c, 77
b, 78 c, 80, 82 l & r, 110 r,
133, 151.

Lars Wiberg
Pour Quoi
Nodre Frihavnsgade 13
2100 Copenhagen
Denmark
t: + 45 35 26 62 54
Pages 5 c, 9, 14 l, 20 ar, 48 l,
54 r, 60, 62 r, 74 c, 88–89,
101, 108, 109b, 114 r,
142–43, 144 r, 160 al.

Nina Hartmann
e: ninahg@tele2.se
www.vintagebynina.com
Pages 2, 4 a, 5 b, 25, 46 al,
46 br, 50 c, 52, 66–67, 75, 78
r, 104, 111, 121, 122 l, 124,
134–35 l.

Marijke van Nunen Interieur
Friezelaan 139
The Netherlands
t: + 31 134 681900
m: + 31 655 825663
e: marijkevannunen@hetnet.nl
Pages 3, 10–11, 12 br, 15 l,
18 l, 23, 26 r, 40–41, 50 l,
54 l, 54 c, 61 c, 73 c, 74l, 99
l & c, 106r, 109 a, 140 l & r,
146–47, 148 l.

Melin Tregwynt
Castlemorris
Haverfordwest
Pembrokeshire
SA62 5UX
t: + 44 (0)1348 891644
e: info@melintregwynt.co.uk
www.melintregwynt.co.uk
Page 14.

Michael Bains and Catherine
Woram
t: + 44 (0)20 8672 3680
Michael@mbainbs.demon.co.uk
Catherine@cworam.demon.co.uk
www.catherineworam.co.uk
Page 71 r.

Naja Lauf A/S
Strandvejen 340
DK-2930 Klampenborg
t: + 45 70 25 13 25
www.najalauf.dk
Page 16 ac.

Ole Lynggaard Copenhagen
Hellerupvej 1 5 B
DK–2900 Hellerup
Denmark
t: + 45 39 46 03 00
www.olelynggaard.dk
Pages 87, 145 l.

Piet Boon Studio
Ambacht 6
1511 JZ Oustzaan
The Netherlands
e: info@pietboon.nl
www.pietboon.nl
Pages 28-29, 49 b, 63 r, 96 l
& c, 99 r, 107 l, 114 l, 126 r,
138, 144 l, 148 r.

Rose Uniacke
8 Holbein Place
London SW1W 8NL, UK
t: + 44 (0)20 7730 7050
e: mail@roseuniacke.com
www.roseuniacke.com
Pages 4 b, 26 l, 38 b, 42 c,
44 r, 45 r, 49 a, 74 r, 79, 85,
153.

Susan Chalom
Options
480 Park Avenue
New York, NY 10022, USA
t: + 212 486 9207
f: + 212 486 8682
susan@susanchalom.com
www.susanchalom.com
Page 39.

Teed Interiors Ltd
for Sasha Waddell Fabrics &
Furniture
t: 020 8979 9189
www.sashawaddell.com
Pages 30, 36, 42 r, 51, 62 l,
64, 84 l, 90-91, 98, 110 c,
112, 119.

www.castlesinthesand.com
t: + 44 (0)776 8352190
(UK mobile)
m: + 44 (0)679 65386
(Moroccan mobile)
For commissions, email
emma@castlesinthesand.com
Pages 140 c, 149.

INDEX

Note: Page numbers in italics refer to captions.

ACKNOWLEDGMENTS

First I would love to thank Lisa Cohen for taking such amazing pictures and for all her inspiration and support throughout the project. Thanks also to all the wonderful assistants who helped us, for all their hard work. Another huge thank you goes to Katherine Sorrell for writing such lovely text.

  Also I want to thank the lovely team at Ryland Peters and Small for all their hard work in making this book possible. Especially Alison Starling, Leslie Harrington, Jess Walton and Pamela Daniels for their continual support and guidance and to everyone who allowed us to photograph their beautiful homes.

  Finally, thank you to my family and friends, especially Andrew for being so supportive and patient.

Kate French

The publisher would also like to thank Tove Westling at Day, Birger et Mikkelsen and Helene Schjerbeck, whose help was greatly appreciated.